KERYGMA

DISCOVERING the BIBLE

RESOURCE BOOK
by KENNETH CLARK

edited by BOYD LIEN

the KERYGMA
program

Art: Boyd Lien

Layout and Design: Kathy Boykowycz

Special thanks to Rev. Sharolyn Welton for her contributions to the original draft of *Kerygma: Discovering the Bible* and to the Tuesday morning class at St. John's Cathedral, Albuquerque, New Mexico. Thanks also to Dr. Donald Griggs, Dr. John Mehl, Ms. Barbara Minges and Dr. D. Cambell Wyckoff for their contributions to the finished publication of this Resource Book.

Grateful acknowledgment is made to the publishers listed below for permission to reprint the following copyrighted material: Discovery 1-Excerpt from *The Oxford Concise Concordance to the Revised Standard Version of the Holy Bible* by Bruce M. Metzger and Isobel M. Metzger. Copyright © 1962 by Oxford University Press, Inc. Reprinted by permission. Discovery 11-Excerpt on Ezekiel 37:1-14 from *Harper's Bible Commentary* by William Neil. Copyright © 1962 by Hodder and Stoughton Ltd. Reprinted by permission of Harper and Row, Publishers, Inc. Discovery 12-Excerpts from the *Illustrated Bible Handbook* by Edward P. Blair. Copyright © 1987 by Abingdon Press, Reprinted by permission. The chronology for the time-line and the maps Egypt and Sinai (Discovery 6), Division of Canaan (Discovery 7), and The Kingdoms of Israel and Judah (Discovery 9) are from the *Good News Bible*. © The United Bible Societies, 1978 and American Bible Society, 1976. Used with permission.

Kerygma: Discovering the Bible is published and distributed by The Kerygma Program, 300 Mt. Lebanon Boulevard, Suite 205, Pittsburgh, PA 15234. Phone 800-537-9462. FAX 412-344-1823. Pennsylvania residents may call collect.

ISBN 1-882236-04-1

theKERYGMA
program

300 Mt. Lebanon Blvd. Pittsburgh, Pennsylvania 15234

Contents

Contents

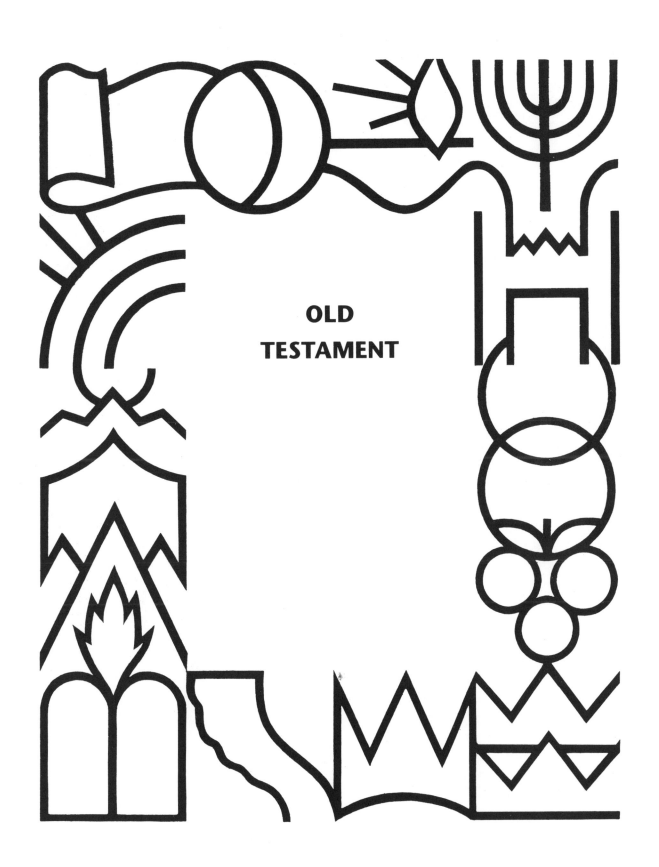

OLD
TESTAMENT

Contents

Preface

WELCOME!

Welcome to *Kerygma: Discovering the Bible.* As you begin this course of study
you will be joining thousands of others throughout the world who make up
the learning community of the Kerygma Program. It is a community where
serious intent, personal preparation and active involvement provide the
basis for significant learning.

Kerygma: Discovering the Bible is a basic comprehensive introduction to the
Bible as a whole. The phrase "The Bible as a Whole" is used to convey a concern for more than learning about each book and its contents. It seeks to
underscore an interest in seeing the inter-connections among the many
parts of the entire Bible, as it speaks to us of God and faith and people.
Through a process of reading, reflection, discussion and creative expression
you will discover people, events and places and encounter a variety of biblical ideas. While the focus of the course is to provide an introduction to the
Bible as a whole, our hope and expectation is that you will move beyond
learning details about people, events and places to new understandings and
experiences of faith and life.

As you begin your study there are two important factors you will want to
keep in mind.

1. Personal preparation is essential to the success of your learning experience. While the time spent with your study group will offer a variety of
learning experiences, the course is based upon the readings from the Bible

that are to be completed before the group meets. During the group meeting you will be sharing the discoveries and questions that arise from your readings.

2. Any introduction to the Bible has built-in frustrations. One of the major frustrations is related to the limitations of time. Some readings will raise more questions than answers. Other readings may trigger ideas that invite further exploration. Occasionally there may not be enough time to raise all of your questions or to explore some of your ideas. So be patient with yourself, the study resources, your leader and others in the group. Hopefully this course of study will be followed by additional study opportunities where questions and ideas introduced here can be explored in greater depth.

KERYGMA: DISCOVERING THE BIBLE – WHAT? WHY? HOW?

The two primary resources for this course are the Bible and this Resource Book.

THE BIBLE

The major resource for *Kerygma: Discovering the Bible* is the Bible. In thirty sessions, you will read many of the key passages in the Bible: verses and chapters, poems and stories, histories and prophecies. Since the Bible unfolds the story of the people of God in a particular order, we will follow that order most of the time.

A study Bible with cross references, footnotes, annotations, and so on, is recommended. A number of good study Bibles are available, such as the *New Oxford Annotated Bible with Apocrypha (RSV)*, *The New English Bible with Apocrypha* (Oxford Study Edition), and the *New Jerusalem Bible* (hardbound with notes). Although it is not a study Bible, many people have found *Today's English Version (Good News Bible)*, published by the American Bible Society, to be a very readable translation.

The translation used in the text of the Resource Book is the *New Revised Standard Version* (except where noted), but you are encouraged to compare it with other contemporary translations. However, the use of a paraphrase is *not* appropriate in a study such as this, where the objective is to come as close to the original text as possible. Since a paraphrase often includes the understanding the translator has of the text, theology and commentary creep in.

THE RESOURCE BOOK

This Resource Book is your guide for reading the Bible. You will use it to help you discover the biblical story and reflect upon its meaning. The biblical story unfolds in thirty sessions – fifteen Old Testament and fifteen New Testament Discoveries. It is essential that you read the material in the Resource Book and complete the suggested activities prior to each session.

The group sessions will build upon the work that has been done in the Resource Book. It will be difficult to be a part of these sessions without having done the individual study, because the group sessions do not rely upon a lecture, but instead depend upon the participants sharing their summaries of the Bible passages as well as the other skill-building activities. The Resource Book and Bible contain everything necessary to prepare you for active participation in the group sessions.

Each Discovery session follows the same format:

1. **The Story Continues.** This section continues the narrative from where it left off in the previous session and summarizes the scope of the biblical story disclosed in the Bible passages for this session. The section begins with a biblical quotation. Many of these quotations are questions, linking us to our ancestors who also sought to know more and who asked questions to discover God's word.

2. **Preparing for the Search.** This is a very important part of your preparation. In this section are the names of people, events, and places you need to know about as you read the passages of scripture listed for the Discovery. Also listed are terms and concepts that will help clarify what you read. At the bottom of the first full pages of each Discovery you will find a "time-line." It indicates when the central events in the biblical story occurred. The early dates are approximate and have been taken from the chronology chart found in *Today's English Version.*

3. **The Search Begins.** Discovery is a search, a process of putting the pieces together. The scripture readings are the most important part of the discovery process. The passages selected to be read in this course are primary texts for understanding the Bible. As you read you are to make notes that will help you summarize the biblical story or the passages.

   In order to keep the preparation time as uniform as possible for each of the Discoveries, care has been taken to balance the number of verses read for each session. The Old Testament sessions, because of the greater number of books, average 180 verses each session; the New Testament sessions average 135 verses. Even so, you will find it difficult to read only the required passages. You may want to read some of the verses that precede and follow these passages. Since there are various ways to tell a story, some selections reflect a choice between parallel readings.

4. **The Search Continues.** The format of this course encourages questions and discoveries; it is an approach intended to engage you and others in the group in a living dialogue with the people of the Bible. Ancient questions are still pondered today. Ancient discoveries provide answers to our search for God.

If we read the Bible expecting to hear God speaking to us, we will discover the voice of the Almighty. Yet, because these ancient writings reflect a world far different from our own, there are many questions that arise from our reading. In other words, both exclamation points and question marks will be key parts of our reading and study of the Bible.

5. **Focusing the Search.** In addition to providing an introductory survey of the Bible, this course introduces or reviews basic Bible study skills. In this section you learn about the use of study tools such as a Bible concordance, Bible dictionary, Bible atlas, Bible handbook, Bible commentary, cross reference notes, footnotes, etc. You will find these skills useful every time you read the Bible.

6. **Putting It Together.** During the discovery process there come "aha!" moments, times when things come together. Those moments may happen to you during your reading of the Bible, in the process of discovering and questioning, in the experience of "focusing the search," or in the activities suggested in this section. These learning activities are broad in scope, taking in the big picture of the biblical story.

7. **Reflection.** After "aha!" comes "so what?" What difference does this discovery make in your life? In what way has God's ancient word become God's current word to you? The purpose for reading the Bible is to discover not only how God has acted and spoken in the past but also to hear what God says to us today. We read the Bible with the assurance that God will make the ancient word spoken to our ancestors a contemporary word spoken to us. Two reflection topics and various questions are provided in this section to guide your personal reflection and prayer.

THE KERYGMA PROGRAM

Kerygma is a Greek word. Originally it meant the proclamation of a herald or government official who made state announcements and bore messages of importance between rulers. The early Christian Church gave the Greek word a new meaning, and in the New Testament the word *kerygma* is used to indicate the content of the message announced by the church. *Kerygma* has since been variously translated as "proclamation" or "preaching" or "word proclaimed."

The Kerygma Program is a publisher of adult Bible study resources that serves a broad ecumenical constituency. It is founded on the conviction that the Church of Jesus Christ has a profoundly important religious heritage. The Church discovers both its origin and its future in the story of the faith and life of God's people as presented in the Bible. The Kerygma Program believes that the most vital communities of faith are formed by people who share the biblical story. To mature in one's faith and life as a Christian requires knowledge of the story, as well as the ability to translate that story to the living of one's life.

There are several distinguishing characteristics of the Kerygma Program:

1. The Kerygma Program's approach to the study of the Bible is comprehensive and holistic. There are two foundational courses in the Kerygma Program – *Kerygma: Discovering the Bible* and *Kerygma: The Bible in Depth.* Neither is a book-by-book approach, nor a literary or doctrinal study. Both courses focus on the "big picture" rather than the small details. Both courses are holistic in that they seek to emphasize the unity in the biblical message and the relationships among all parts of the Bible. Both courses are not just studies about the Bible but demand a direct involvement with the Bible through reading, searching, questioning, sharing, and reflecting.

   This course, *Kerygma: Discovering the Bible,* is a basic introduction to the Bible. In thirty sessions the biblical story is told from beginning to end, from God's creation of the universe to God's promise of a new creation. The purpose of *Kerygma: Discovering the Bible* is to provide a course of study for two categories of adults; those who have little experience reading and studying the Bible and those who may have participated in some study groups but have never looked at the Bible as a whole. The focus of this study is to enable adults to gain a familiarity with the people, events, places, and ideas within the Bible and to discover the interrelationships of the parts of Scripture.

Kerygma: The Bible in Depth is an ideal way to continue discovering the Bible. Its most unique feature is a thematic approach to the Bible. The value of this approach is that it gives a "whole-Bible" grasp of what is more often studied piecemeal. The ten themes, which involve the interaction between God and people in both the Old and New Testaments, are not imposed on the Bible nor on its study. Rather, they arise from the Bible itself and confront us as we read and explore the texts.

2. The Kerygma Program's approach to the study of the Bible is both historical and contemporary, providing means for us to hear and participate in the biblical story. In *Kerygma: Discovering the Bible,* the biblical story is read, summarized, and discussed from the vantage point of the people of God who lived it. The questions and discoveries that arise from the biblical story are the links between then and now. The study is completed by discovering the significance of the biblical story in the lives and community of the people of God today.

3. The Kerygma Program's approach to the study of the Bible in this resource is incomplete. The process of "Discovering the Bible" is completed only when, and to the degree that, the transforming message of the Bible becomes manifest in the faith and life of the people who participate in the study. The objective of the Kerygma Program is not simply to increase biblical literacy, but to infuse biblical faith into the lives of individuals and communities. The objective is similar to the statement found near the end of the Gospel of John: "But these are written so that you may come to believe that Jesus is the Messiah, the Son of God, and that through believing you may have life in his name." (John 20:31)

The symbol for *The Search* is the open Bible with the descending dove (the Holy Spirit) kindling the reader's understanding.

The Search

THE STORY BEGINS

O LORD, you have searched me and known me. Where can I go from your spirit? Or where can I flee from your presence? Search me, O God, and know my heart; test me and know my thoughts. Psalm 139:1,7,23

Our purpose, and our greatest hope, is to discover the Bible, and within the Bible to discover the God who is revealed – the God who speaks to us in its pages, who calls to us in its stories, and who thus searches us out.

On the surface it may appear that humanity's search for God is a major theme in the Bible. Yet, as we begin to discover the Bible we become aware that it is primarily a story of God's search, not ours. The human story in the Bible is often the story of those who avoid the search for God – or, once they embark upon it, either abandon the search or go off in a different direction. The divine story in the Bible is the story of creation and recreation, of calling and restoration, of blessing and forgiveness, of empowering leaders, kings, prophets, until ultimately God comes in Jesus Christ. Clearly, the major theme that runs throughout the Bible from Genesis to Revelation is God's ceaseless search for humanity.

Yes, the image of discovery has two sides to it: God is seeking us even as we seek God. Therefore, our purpose in discovering the Bible is not simply to study ancient documents, but to meet the God who "created the heavens and the earth" and "loved the world so much that he gave his only Son." As we begin our course, *Kerygma: Discovering the Bible,* it is God who guides and inspires our discoveries so that we may seek and find.

PREPARING FOR THE SEARCH

This is a very important part of your preparation. In this section are the names of people, events, and places you need to know about as you read the passages of Scripture listed for the Discovery. Also listed are terms and concepts that help clarify what you read.

Bible means books. It is an English word that comes from the Old French word *bible*, which was a translation of the Latin and Greek words *biblia*, meaning books. The word applies to the 66 books of the Christian Scriptures, or the 39 books of the Jewish Scriptures.

Kingdom of Heaven is the term Matthew often uses in place of the Kingdom of God. The phrase literally means the reign or rule of God and is a central theme of the New Testament.

Sheol (shay'ohl) may refer to either the depths of the earth or the gloomy underworld of departed spirits. (Psalm 139:8)

Testament is from the Latin word *testamentum*, meaning a will or agreement, or more specifically a covenant, in the sense of God's covenant with Abraham and Sarah. In Christian Bibles it is commonly used for the thirty-nine books of the Hebrew Scriptures of the Old Testament and the twenty-seven books of the New Testament.

THE SEARCH BEGINS

As you prepare for each session, spend most of your time reading the selected passages of Scripture that provide you with the necessary background to understand one part of the biblical "story." The purpose of this introductory session is to help you become familiar with the format and design of the course. Each SEARCH leads you to DISCOVERY – discovery about the history of the people of God; discovery about how God acts in the lives of people and nations; discovery about the ways God has been and is active in your life.

As you read these passages pay close attention to the theme of search . In each of the following sessions, you are invited to take part in the retelling of the story. The notes that you make will enable you to do this. *Therefore, preparation is essential!*

BCE	c. 1900		1250	1210
	Patriarchs Abraham Isaac Jacob Joseph		**the** **Exodus** Moses Aaron Miriam	**the** **Conquest** **and** **Settlement** Joshua the Judges Samuel

No one is going to check your notes, so feel free to use your own short-hand. Use these questions to guide your reading.

- *Who is doing the seeking? Who is found?*
- *Each writer brings a different perspective about the relationship between God and humankind. With which one do you most identify?*

Psalm 139: 1–24, Search Me, O God

Isaiah 55:1–13, Seek the Lord

Matthew 13:44–46, Hidden Treasure

1030	930		722/721	587/586	538	333	63
Monarchy Founded	**Divided Kingdom**	Elisha	**Fall of Samaria**	**Fall of Jerusalem**	**Return and Restoration**	**Greek Rule**	**Roman Rule**
Saul	Jeroboam	Jehu	Josiah	**Exile in**	Haggai	Daniel	
David	Rehoboam	Amos	Zephaniah	**Babylon**	Zechariah	written	
Solomon	Ahab	Hosea		Ezekiel	Ezra		
	Elijah	Micah			Nehemiah		
		1 Isaiah					

LUKE 11:1–13, Ask, Seek, Knock

ACTS 17:22–28, All Seek God

THE SEARCH CONTINUES

Reading the Bible makes us ask questions. Some of the questions deal with who, what, where, and when. "Who wrote: the book of Acts? When was it written?" This type of question can usually be answered either from information within the group or with a little research in a Bible dictionary, handbook, or commentary. Other questions, the type not so easily answered, have to do with *why* and *how*. "Why does God tolerate unfaithfulness? How can everyone who 'asks' receive?" Some of these questions cannot be answered with finality. Record in the space below the questions that arise as you read. Not all of your questions can be answered during the session, but as you continue through the course many of them will be resolved.

In these readings I have questions about...

As we read carefully, we make discoveries. Some discoveries are factual. "I discovered that God's people were unfaithful when Deuteronomy was written." On the other hand, discoveries may be profound. These discoveries have an "aha" quality about them. "I discovered that God's faithfulness doesn't depend on my faithfulness. God really cares about me!" Record your discoveries – the profound and the not so profound. All discoveries are valuable!

In these readings I discovered...

FOCUSING THE SEARCH

This section of each Discovery introduces new Bible study skills or reinforces those you have already learned. Since responsible Bible study involves more than reading Scripture, you learn about the use of study tools such as a Bible concordance, Bible dictionary, Bible atlas, Bible handbook, Bible commentary, cross reference notes, footnotes, etc. Often this skill will be reviewed during the session. However, since session time is limited, occasionally this material is not discussed. Nevertheless, these skills enable you to become a better student of the Bible.

The passages you read in "The Search Begins" emphasized the words *seek* or *search*. You may have wondered how those passages were selected. How does an author know where to find verses that fit a specific topic – in this case seeking or searching? There is no great mystery. In spite of what some people think, most Bible "experts" have not memorized thousands and thousands of Bible texts. Instead, when they need to locate a passage on a particular theme they turn to a study tool called a Bible **concordance.** There are two major types of concordances.

> An **exhaustive concordance** provides a *complete* alphabetical listing of *all* the words found in the Bible with references to all the passages in which they occur.

For most purposes, however, a **concise concordance** is sufficient. A *concise concordance* provides an alphabetical listing of *important words* found in the Bible with references to *selected* passages in which they occur.

Many study Bibles have a concordance in the back. Check to see if yours does. If you decide to purchase a concordance, remember to buy a concordance that is published for the translation of the Bible you use.

Below is an entry from *The Oxford Concise Concordance to the Revised Standard Version of the Holy Bible.* In it you will find the word SEEK. Read the first line below the word. The letter s stands for the word seek in that phrase. The notation Dt.4:29 means that this reference is in the book of Deuteronomy, the fourth chapter, verse 29. Select two or three other passages listed under SEEK and read them. Are they ones that might have been used in this session? Why or why not?

SEEK

from there you will *s.* the Lord your	Dt.4.29	return and *s.* the Lord their God	Hos.3.5
have set your heart to *s.* God	2 Chr.19.3	*S.* the Lord and live, lest he break	Am.5.6
never *s.* their peace or prosperity	Ezra 9.12	*S.* good, and not evil, that you may	Am.5.14
I would *s.* God, and to God would I	Job 5.8	*S.* the Lord, all you humble of the	Zeph.2.3
the generation of those who *s.* him	Ps.24.6	But *s.* first his kingdom and his	Mt.6.33
Thou hast said, "*S.* ye my face."	Ps.27.8	*s.*, and you will find; knock, and	Mt.7.7
In thee, O Lord, do I *s.* refuge	Ps.31.1	Why do you *s.* the living among the	Lk.24.5
do good; *s.* peace, and pursue it	Ps.34.14	I *s.* not my own will but	Jn.5.30
S. the Lord and his strength	Ps.105.4	You will *s.* me and you will not find	Jn.7.36
I applied my mind to *s.* and to	Ec.1.13	they should *s.* God, in the hope	Acts 17.27
a time to *s.*, and a time to lose	Ec.3.6	demand signs and Greeks *s.* wisdom	1 Cor.1.22
s. justice, correct oppression	Is.1.17	Let no one *s.* his own good	1 Cor.10.24
S. the Lord while he may be found	Is.55.6	*s.* the things that are above, where	Col.3.1
when you *s.* me with all your heart	Jer.29.13	nor did we *s.* glory from men	1 Th.2.6
do you *s.* great things for yourself?	Jer.45.5	that he rewards those who *s.* him	Heb.11.6
they will *s.* peace, but there shall	Ezek.7.25	let him *s.* peace and pursue it	1 Pet.3.11
I will *s.* the lost, and I will	Ezek.34.16		

PUTTING IT TOGETHER

This section of the Resource Book attempts to help you fit the pieces of the Discovery together. This is accomplished in a variety of ways, but one thing is always constant. You are asked to do something in "Putting It Together" that will be useful during the session. Again, preparation is an important part of this course!

Since this is probably your first opportunity to look at the Resource Book, you could not have completed any preparation for this session. By now you may even be wondering how you are going to find time to prepare for future sessions. This is a legitimate concern. The leader of your group will want to address this question. Alone or with a partner come up with two or three plans of action that will help you set aside the time you will need. Write your ideas here. You will be asked to share them with the group.

REFLECTION

The word reflect means to think or consider seriously. In this section you are asked to reflect on questions that help you take an in-depth look at some of the passages or at yourself. What you write here does not need to be shared with others, although there are times when you will have an opportunity to do so, if you are willing.

1. Think about your own search to know God. What are you hoping to have happen to you as a result of this course, *Kerygma: Discovering the Bible?* What commitments will you make in order to make that happen?

2. Reflect upon the discovery process. What are some important discoveries that you have made in your life? In what ways did those discoveries take place?

The symbol for *The Scriptures* is a scroll, the form in which the Scriptures were first written.

The Scriptures

THE STORY CONTINUES

They said to each other, "Were not our hearts burning within us while he was talking to us on the road, while he was opening the scriptures to us? Luke 24:32

Although it is appropriate to use the terms Scriptures and Bible interchangeably, the title of this session refers only to the books of the Old Testament. In fact, when the term "the Scriptures" appears in the New Testament, the author means those books accepted at that time as "sacred writings." By the time of Jesus this collection included the *Law* (Genesis, Exodus, Leviticus, Numbers, Deuteronomy), the *Prophets* (which in the Hebrew tradition included the books from Joshua through 2 Kings, excluding Ruth, as well as what we call the Prophets), and the *Psalms.* Although the other books that are now part of our Old Testament were in use at that time, they were not included in the *canon* or official list of authoritative Scriptures, until approximately 90 A.D.

This use of the word "Scriptures" is especially clear in an episode from Jesus' life. On Easter Sunday the risen Jesus joins two disciples walking from Jerusalem to Emmaus. As they walk together Jesus interprets his death and resurrection by explaining the Scriptures to them, beginning with the Law of Moses and continuing with the Prophets. God speaks to the disciples in the words of the Scriptures and causes their hearts to burn with understanding and joy!

Long before 90 A.D., however, the Scriptures were treasured as the sacred writings, the inspired Word of God. In this session on the Scriptures and in the following thirteen sessions on the Old Testament we discover the Bible Jesus knew and used.

Out of ancient literature, why these books in particular? We believe that they are God's self-revelation, that through them the unique and authoritative Word of God is spoken to us. They are instruments of God's search for us. At the same time, as we read, study, and interpret them, we are seeking to understand God's reality, nature, and will. They are instruments for our search.

PREPARING FOR THE SEARCH

The thirty-nine books of our Old Testament are grouped together as the Law, the Historical Books, the Poetry and Wisdom, and the Prophets. This explains why the material in the Old Testament is not in chronological order, a fact you may have discovered if you have tried to read the Bible from Genesis to Malachi. This adds to our difficulty as we study the Bible. Therefore it is essential to understand these groupings and be able to identify which books belong in each category.

The following quotation is important to keep in mind as you read the information below.

> The exact contents of the Bible and the arrangement of its books have varied considerably in different places and periods of Jewish and Christian history. *Illustrated Bible Handbook,* p. 17.

Law. The Pentateuch (Greek, for five scrolls) or Torah (Hebrew for the law), is comprised of the first five books of the Old Testament: Genesis, Exodus, Leviticus, Numbers, and Deuteronomy.

History. These books tell the story of Israel as a nation. They are not historical in the usual sense, although much of what they include is of interest to historians. Joshua, Judges, (Ruth), 1 and 2 Samuel (1 and 2 indicate that two scrolls were needed to contain the material), 1 and 2 Kings, (1 and 2 Chronicles, Ezra, Nehemiah, and Esther) are often more like preaching than what we have come to expect in books of history. All of these, except those in parentheses, are called the Former Prophets in the Hebrew Canon. Those in parentheses are included in the Writings.

BCE	c. 1900		1250	1210
	Patriarchs Abraham Isaac Jacob Joseph		**the** **Exodus** Moses Aaron Miriam	**the** **Conquest** **and** **Settlement** Joshua the Judges Samuel

Poetry and Wisdom. The Hebrews, like others in similar cultures, made wide use of poetic forms, which was considered a proper way to celebrate victories, make important declarations about national policy, and worship God. In fact nearly one third of the Old Testament is poetic material, and most of the material in the books classified as poetry and wisdom is poetic in nature. The books in these categories include Job, Psalms, Proverbs, Ecclesiastes, and Song of Solomon (also called Song of Songs). Except for most of Psalms and all of Song of Solomon, these books contain "wisdom literature." Wisdom literature is either of a philosophical nature (like Job and Ecclesiastes) or consists of practical wisdom (like Proverbs), used for moral instruction. In Hebrew Scripture these books were included in the Writings.

Prophets (Major/Minor). This list includes Isaiah, Jeremiah, Ezekiel, Hosea, Joel, Amos, Obadiah, Jonah, Micah, Nahum, Habbakuk, Zephaniah, Haggai, Zechariah, and Malachi. From at least 430 A.D. Isaiah, Jeremiah, and Ezekiel are called the "major" prophets because of the length of the books bearing their names. The remaining twelve, all of which fit on one scroll, are called the "minor" prophets. Major and minor refer only to length and *not* to content. In Hebrew Scripture these books are called the Latter Prophets. Lamentations, which follows Jeremiah in the Protestant Bible, was placed there because in some ancient translations the words "of Jeremiah" were added to the title. Daniel, which follows Ezekiel, and Lamentations are included in the books called Writings in Hebrew Scripture.

Scripture comes from the Latin word for "writing." Many such writings existed; the ones that were accepted into the Old Testament were those which had been used by the community for worship and devotion and had gained favor. "The Scriptures" is a name given to the writings accepted into the canon, the authoritative list of books.

Scrolls. In ancient times writing was done by hand on long strips of material made of either papyrus or specially prepared leather called parchment. Wooden or metal rods were attached to each end of the strips and the material was rolled around the rods. To read a "book" of Scripture one would unroll the papyrus or parchment to the desired place, picking up the slack on the other rod. In Hebrew synagogues and temples scrolls are still used.

Writings. In the Hebrew Bible the books in this category include Psalms, Job, Proverbs, Ruth, Song of Songs (Song of Solomon), Qoheleth (Ecclesiastes), Lamentations, Esther, Daniel, Ezra-Nehemiah (one scroll), and Chronicles.

1030	930		722/721	587/586	538	333	63
Monarchy Founded	**Divided Kingdom**	Elisha	**Fall of Samaria**	**Fall of Jerusalem**	**Return and Restoration**	**Greek Rule**	**Roman Rule**
Saul	Jeroboam	Jehu	Josiah	**Exile in**	Haggai	Daniel	
David	Rehoboam	Amos	Zephaniah	**Babylon**	Zechariah	written	
Solomon	Ahab	Hosea		Ezekiel	Ezra		
	Elijah	Micah			Nehemiah		
		1 Isaiah					

THE SEARCH BEGINS

To begin your search, read the following representative passages in your Bible and write a short summary of each one. Most of these passages will be read again in later discoveries. As you read the passages this time, try to identify some characteristics of the type of literature they represent. Although the notes you make are for your own use, you will refer to them when the group gathers to share information about *The Scriptures*.

THE LAW (Genesis to Deuteronomy)

Deuteronomy 6:4–9, The Great Commandment

Exodus 20:1–17, The Ten Commandments

THE HISTORICAL BOOKS: (Joshua to Esther)

1 Samuel 16:1–13, Samuel Anoints David

1 Kings 19:1–21, Elijah on Mount Sinai

THE POETRY AND WISDOM: (Job to Song of Songs)

Job 28:12–28, Wisdom is Praised

Psalm 145, Praise the Lord

THE PROPHETS: (Isaiah to Malachi)

Isaiah 6:1–13, The Call of Isaiah

Jeremiah 7:1–15, God's Judgment on the Nation

THE SEARCH CONTINUES

In these readings I have questions about...

In these readings I discovered...

FOCUSING THE SEARCH

Long before many parts of the Bible were written down and became known as "Scripture" (which means "writing") they were told as stories, spoken as prayers, and recited as poetry. They were told, remembered, and retold, often for hundreds of years.

When the Scriptures were put into writing, most of the various "books" were written on papyrus or parchment scrolls. Today we read from books rather than scrolls, and unless we read Hebrew, we read the Scriptures in an English translation of the ancient text that has survived and been preserved.

Use the following worksheet, "The Scriptures In Translation," to examine both the Hebrew and English texts of Genesis 15:6–7 and the process of translation.

THE SCRIPTURES IN TRANSLATION

Genesis 15:6-7,

The language of the Old Testament is Hebrew, a language originally written with consonants alone. The vowels, which are the markings you will notice underneath the letters, were added much later. Hebrew is read from right to left. Thus, the English translations below each line are also read from right to left.

Try your hand at being a translator. The two English translations you see below the Hebrew words are from two different "interlinear" (between the lines) translations of the Bible. Use these translations to arrive at your own translation.

Now, look up the passage in your own Bible and write how it has been translated there.

PUTTING IT TOGETHER

The Protestant Bible is a collection of sixty-six[1] books. The thirty-nine books in the Old Testament tell a story encompassing thousands of years, whereas the twenty-seven books in the New Testament cover less than two hundred years of history. Even so, every individual part of the Bible comes together to tell how God deals with us and seeks for us lovingly. This course includes thirty Discoveries. Each tells one part of the ongoing biblical story.

Often as you use your Bible and other resources, you will find that the names of the books of the Bible are abbreviated. Locate in the front of your Bible the page that lists the names of the books and their abbreviations. Fill in the 39 abbreviations on the chart below. Listed next to the abbreviation are the numbers of the Discoveries in this course which focus on that book of the Bible.

NOTE

[1]Some study Bibles include books known as the Apocrypha or Deuterocanonicals. These fifteen books were written in the years called the "intertestamental" period. Although they are not part of the Hebrew Scriptures, they cover an important time in the life of the people of God. When included in a Protestant Bible, these books are usually inserted after the end of the Old Testament.

THE OLD TESTAMENT SCRIPTURES

Literature	Book	Abbreviation	Discovery
Law	Genesis	_____	2, 3, 4
	Exodus	_____	2, 5, 6, 13
	Leviticus	_____	
	Numbers	_____	6
	Deuteronomy	_____	6, 13

Literature	Book	Abbreviation	Discovery
History	Joshua	_____	7
	Judges	_____	7
	Ruth	_____	12
	1 Samuel	_____	2, 7, 8
	2 Samuel	_____	8
	1 Kings	_____	2, 8, 9
	2 Kings	_____	9
	1 Chronicles	_____	
	2 Chronicles	_____	
	Ezra	_____	12
	Nehemiah	_____	12
	Esther	_____	
Poetry/Wisdom	Job	_____	2, 14
	Psalms	_____	1, 2, 13, 14
	Proverbs	_____	14
	Ecclesiastes	_____	14
	Song of Solomon	_____	
Prophets	Isaiah	_____	1,10, 11, 12
	Jeremiah	_____	2, 11
	Lamentations	_____	
	Ezekiel	_____	11
	Daniel	_____	15
	Hosea	_____	10
	Joel	_____	15
	Amos	_____	10
	Obadiah	_____	

Literature	Book	Abbreviation	Discovery
Prophets cont.	Jonah	_____	12
	Micah	_____	10
	Nahum	_____	
	Habakkuk	_____	
	Zephaniah	_____	15
	Haggai	_____	
	Zechariah	_____	15
	Malachi	_____	15

REFLECTION

1. Reflect upon God's gift of the Scriptures. In what ways has God spoken to you in the Bible? When has the Bible filled you with understanding and joy? What are some stories or verses that have a special meaning to you?

2. When asked to answer the question, "What is the Bible?" some people respond, "The Bible is the Word of God, (the message of love and redemption)." Others believe that the Bible contains the literal "words of God." Reflect on these two ideas. How do you answer the question, "What is the Bible?"

The symbol for *The Beginnings* is a rainbow, God's sign of the covenant with Noah. (Genesis 9:12–13)

The Beginnings

THE STORY CONTINUES

In the beginning when God created the heavens and the earth, the earth was a formless void and darkness covered the face of the deep, while a mighty wind swept over the face of the waters.
Genesis 1:1, 2

What a simple, yet profound, way to begin telling the story of God's creation. The Bible begins with the affirmation that our universe, our world, and we ourselves are the creation of God.

The stories in Genesis, the book of beginnings, provide the framework for all that follows in the biblical story: God creates, God communicates, God promises, God judges, God commands, and most importantly, God saves. For the framework rests upon the firm foundation that God, the creator of the universe, is also the one who saves the people of Israel from slavery in Egypt and delivers them in the Exodus.

The stories in Genesis 1–11, our focus in this discovery, add crucial details to the framework: God is almighty, creation is good, humanity bears God's image, sin exists, God punishes evil. In the story of Noah, for instance, God saves the faithful and promises a future.

PREPARING FOR THE SEARCH

Listed below you will find the names of people, places, and terms that are important in *The Beginnings*. Read these definitions now. They will help as you read the Scripture passages in "The Search Begins."

Abel, whose name is derived from the Hebrew for "son," was the second son of Adam and Eve. A shepherd, he was judged righteous when God accepted his offering of a lamb. Abel died at the hand of Cain, his older brother. (Genesis 4:1–8)

Adam is the Hebrew word for "human being" or "mankind," whom God created as male and female. It is also the name given to the first human, the father of the human race, and the father of Cain, Abel, and Seth. (Genesis 2:4 to 5:5)

Babel (ba' buhl), a predecessor of Babylon, was the name of the city in which a tower was built to reach the heavens on the plain of Shinar (ancient Sumer). The name may be a word play on the Hebrew word for "confuse" because of the confusion caused by the many languages. (Genesis 10:10; Genesis 11:1–9)

Cain was the oldest son of Adam and Eve. A farmer, he was not judged righteous when God rejected his gift of produce. Cain killed his brother Abel and was exiled to the land of Nod, east of Eden. (Genesis 4:1–26)

Cherubim is the plural of the Hebrew "cherub." These were the living creatures who guarded the tree of life in Eden. In some ancient sculptures the cherubim are depicted as having the body of a lion, the face of a human, and the wings of an eagle – hardly fitting a notion of cute "cherubs!" (Genesis 3:24)

Covenant. After the flood God promised never to destroy the world again with water. The sign of this covenant was the rainbow. This covenant is a gracious gift of God because the people have no conditions to fulfill. But a covenant is generally formed between two or more parties with obligations for each. (Genesis 6:18; Genesis 9:8–17)

Eden is the name of the pleasant garden (paradise) in which God placed Adam. Its main features besides abundant vegetation are the Tree of Life and the Tree of the Knowledge of Good and Evil. The former tree is probably a symbol for the harmonious existence God willed for humankind. The latter tree became the object of the temptation of Adam and Eve. It symbolized the knowledge or prerogatives that belong to God alone. (Genesis 2:8)

Eve resembles the Hebrew word for living and was the name of the first woman. In Genesis 3:20 she is called the "mother of all living." More specifically Eve was the mother of Cain, Abel, Seth, and other children. (Genesis 2:18 to 4:26)

BCE	c. 1900		1250	1210
	Patriarchs		**the**	**the**
	Abraham		**Exodus**	**Conquest**
	Isaac		Moses	**and**
	Jacob		Aaron	**Settlement**
	Joseph		Miriam	Joshua
				the Judges
				Samuel

Genesis, the first book of the Bible, was given its name from the Greek word for "origins, beginnings." The Hebrew name for the book is "In beginning." Genesis is a book about the beginnings of the human race (Genesis 1–11) and the origin of God's people. (Genesis 12–50)

Noah, a righteous man who lived in an age of wickedness, was delivered when God instructed him to build an ark to save his family and all species of animals from the destruction of the flood. After the flood God made a new covenant with Noah and his family. The sign of this covenant was the rainbow. (Genesis 5:28 to 9:29)

THE SEARCH BEGINS

As you read the passages listed below, you will discover information about *The Beginnings*. The notes you take will help you retell the story to others in your group. These questions can help guide your reading:

- *What did the people of Israel seem to believe about the creation of the world?*
- *What do you think God's purpose was in creating the world?*
- *What do the stories of creation tell us about the nature of God and the nature of humanity?*
- *If God created a good world, why is there evil present in it?*
- *How might we best understand these stories today?*

Genesis 1:1–2:4a, ("a" indicates you are to read only the first half of verse 4)
The Story of Creation

1030	930		722/721	587/586	538	333	63
Monarchy Founded	**Divided Kingdom**	Elisha	**Fall of Samaria**	**Fall of Jerusalem**	**Return and Restoration**	**Greek Rule**	**Roman Rule**
Saul	Jeroboam	Jehu	Josiah	**Exile in Babylon**	Haggai	Daniel written	
David	Rehoboam	Amos	Zephaniah	Ezekiel	Zechariah		
Solomon	Ahab	Hosea			Ezra		
	Elijah	Micah			Nehemiah		
		1 Isaiah					

Genesis 2:4b-25, Another Account of Creation

Genesis 3:1–24, The Temptation of Adam and Eve

Genesis 4:1–16, The Story of Cain and Abel

Genesis 6:5–9:17, The Story of Noah and the Flood

Genesis 11:1–9, The Story of the Tower of Babel

THE SEARCH CONTINUES

In these readings I have questions about...

In these readings I discovered...

FOCUSING THE SEARCH

Often we try to make the Bible into something it was never intended to be.
We are particularly prone to do that with the first eleven chapters of Genesis.
The Bible is a "book about faith" and not a science book. Nowhere in the

Old Testament do the writers try to prove the existence of God. They affirm that God is, and that God creates. And then they go on to tell others about how God has acted in the lives of the people.

As you read the stories listed in "The Search Begins", you may have discovered for the first time that the Bible tells two different stories of creation. Without looking back at your notes or your Bible, write in your own words the story of creation as you remember it. Put in as many details as you can.

Now, open your Bible to Genesis 1:1 and read through 2:4a. As you read, underline or mark with a highlighter everything in your story of creation that comes from this passage. Next, check to see if the remaining material comes from Genesis 2:4b – 25.

What does this exercise seem to indicate about the way we remember biblical stories?

What do both of these creation stories tell us about God?

Why do you think those who put the Bible in its final form included both of these accounts?

PUTTING IT TOGETHER

One of the best ways to understand and appreciate the stories in Genesis 1–11 is to read them as if they contain answers to questions once asked. Just imagine our ancient ancestors contemplating the miracle of life and raising questions about the wonder and meaning of it all. It seems they asked many of the questions we ask today!

Using the chart "The Beginnings: Answers And Questions," take one or more of the stories from Genesis and read it in reverse, so to speak. If the story contains one or more answers, what were the questions? For instance, consider the story of "The Tower of Babel" in Genesis 11:1–9. One of the questions that probably inspired that story is, "Why do we speak different languages?"

THE BEGINNINGS: ANSWERS AND QUESTIONS

Genesis 2:4b-17   answer _____

_____

question _____

_____

Genesis 2:18–24   answer _____

_____

question _____

_____

Genesis 3:1–13   answer _____

_____

question _____

_____

Genesis 3:14–24   answer _____

_____

question _____

_____

Genesis 4:1–16   answer _____

_____

question _____

_____

Genesis 6:1–8   answer _____

_____

question _____

_____

Genesis 11:1–9   answer _____

_____

question _____

_____

REFLECTION

1. Reflect upon the affirmation that men and women were created "in the image of God" (Genesis 1:27). What does it mean to you to be created "in God's image?" In what ways does this belief make a difference in your life?

2. Remember God's delight in creation, "and God saw that it was good" (Genesis 1:10). How have you come to see and discover God's creation as good? In what ways have these stories from Genesis revealed God to you?

The symbol for *The Promise* is a tent representing the ancestors who responded to God's call. (Genesis 12:8)

The Promise

THE STORY CONTINUES

Then Abraham fell on his face and laughed, and said to himself, "Can a child be born to a man who is a hundred years old? Can Sarah, who is ninety years old, bear a child?" Genesis 17:17

The stories of the beginnings are about the creation of the universe, the world, and the whole human race. What about the beginnings of the Hebrews as a distinct people? God calls Abraham to leave his home in Haran and journey toward the west to a new home in Canaan. God's call comes with a promise (or covenant): Abraham and Sarah will be blessed with a child and eventually, through their child and his descendants, the entire world will be blessed.

God's call to Abraham is the beginning of the unique relationship between God and the people of Israel. The chief element in this relationship is a covenant—an agreement, or mutual promise, between God and Israel, in which each assumes an obligation toward the other. At this point the covenant is between God and Abraham—Abraham promises to obey by taking his family to a new land; God promises that Abraham will have many descendants. But at the same time, a covenant community is created, for it is clear that God will maintain a covenant with Abraham's descendants. The covenant becomes a mutual agreement that God will bless them and that they will be faithful and obedient.

Abraham is faithful to God's call, yet somewhat doubtful about God's promise. Even when God confirms the promise and as a sign changes his name from Abram to Abraham, meaning "father of many," he questions the promise and laughs in amazement. But God is faithful to the promise. Abraham and Sarah's son is born. They name him Isaac, meaning "he laughs."

God's promise of children, land, fame, and blessings is the theme connecting the stories of Abraham and Sarah and their descendants. See how the promise is passed from father to son in these passages.

> When Abram was ninety-nine years old the LORD appeared to Abram, and said to him, "I am God Almighty; walk before me, and be blameless. And I will make my covenant between me and you, and will make you exceedingly numerous... As for me, this is my covenant with you: You shall be the ancestor of a multitude of nations... I will establish my covenant between me and you, and your offspring after you throughout their generations, for an ever-lasting covenant, to be God to you and to your offspring after you. And I will give to you and to your offspring after you, the land where you are now an alien, all the land of Canaan, for a perpetual holding; and I will be their God. ...Your wife Sarah shall bear you a son, and you shall name him Isaac. I will establish my covenant with him as an everlasting covenant for his offspring after him." (Genesis 17:1, 2, 4, 7, 8, 19)

> God said to him, "Your name is Jacob; no longer shall you be called Jacob, but Israel shall be your name." So he was called Israel. God said to him, "I am God Almighty: be fruitful and multiply; a nation and a company of nations shall come from you, and kings shall spring from you. The land that I gave to Abraham and Isaac I will give to you, and I will give the land to your offspring after you." (Genesis 35:10–12)

As the stories of Isaac, Jacob, and Joseph unfold, the reader wonders, with Abraham and Sarah, not whether, but how, God will fulfill the promise. Neither Abraham and Sarah's old age, Isaac's near sacrifice, Jacob and Esau's rivalry, Joseph's brothers' treachery, nor a famine in Canaan prevents God from making the promise come true. God is faithful.

BCE	c. 1900		1250	1210
	Patriarchs Abraham Isaac Jacob Joseph		**the Exodus** Moses Aaron Miriam	**the Conquest and Settlement** Joshua the Judges Samuel

PREPARING FOR THE SEARCH

Read about these people, places, and words that have special meaning in *The Promise.*

Abraham, who was first known as Abram, journeyed with his wife Sarai from Ur of the Chaldees by way of Haran to the Land of Canaan to receive the promises of God. When God made the covenant with him, Abram was given the name Abraham, which may be translated from Hebrew as "father of many nations." Abraham's faith in God was strong; he journeyed to a new homeland and later was willing to offer his son Isaac as a sacrifice. (Genesis 11:31–32; 12:1 to 25:11)

Beersheba (beer-shee' bah), a city formed around a well on the desert's edge, was on the southern boundary of Israelite land. The phrase "from Dan to Beersheba" was used to refer to the extent of Israel's land, north to south. Abraham and Jacob were active in and around Beersheba. (Genesis 21:14, 31–32; 26:23–33)

Bethel (beth' uhl), a town twelve miles north of Jerusalem, was given the name which means "house of God" when Jacob had his vision of a ladder of angels. (Genesis 28:10–22) Later, at the time of the two kingdoms, King Jeroboam of Israel set up an altar and golden calf at Bethel. During the exile in the 6th century B.C., it was settled by the Assyrians.

Birthright. According to ancient custom the birthright belonged to the oldest son. This meant he received a double portion of the inheritance. Esau gave up his birthright to Jacob. (Genesis 25:29–34)

Canaan (kay' nan), includes sections of what is now Israel and Lebanon. As part of the Middle East (see the Journey of Abraham map), the area was subject to much conflict.

Circumcision is the removal of the foreskin of the penis of the male infant. The origin of the rite is disputed. It was practiced in several cultures of the ancient Near East. The Hebrews interpreted circumcision as an outward and visible sign of God's covenant. (Genesis 17:11)

Covenant is an agreement between two or more parties in which each assumes some obligation toward the other. The Hebrew word for covenant means "bond" and can refer to a pact between individuals or societies. Most often in the Bible covenant refers to a "bonding" together of God and God's people. The biblical covenants depict God's intense desire to be bonded with humanity. It was God who initiated the covenants with Noah, Abraham,

1030	930		722/721	587/586	538	333	63
Monarchy Founded	**Divided Kingdom**	Elisha	**Fall of Samaria**	**Fall of Jerusalem**	**Return and Restoration**	**Greek Rule**	**Roman Rule**
Saul	Jeroboam	Jehu	Josiah	**Exile in**	Haggai	Daniel	
David	Rehoboam	Amos	Zephaniah	**Babylon**	Zechariah	written	
Solomon	Ahab	Hosea		Ezekiel	Ezra		
	Elijah	Micah			Nehemiah		
		1 Isaiah					

Moses, and David and promised the gifts of life, protection, land, and descendants. It was God who determined the people's appropriate response to the covenants – obedience, circumcision, keeping the Sabbath and the Ten Commandments. It was God who offered the bonding; the covenant is an act of grace.

Edom (ee' duhm), a name which means "red," was given to Esau after he sold his birthright to Jacob for a bowl of red pottage (stew or thick soup). The descendants of Esau were the Edomites who occupied the territory south of the Dead Sea, an area of red sandstone. Even though the Edomites were considered brothers of the Israelites, during most of their history these people were at war with each other. (Genesis 25:30)

Esau (ee' saw), a son of Isaac and Rebecca and twin of Jacob, was a fiery redhead. In fact, his name is a word play on the Hebrew word for "red." Esau, tricked twice by his younger twin Jacob, lost both his birthright and his father's blessing. Esau's descendants became the Edomite ("Red") people. (Genesis 25:21 to 27:41)

Hagar (hay' gahr), Sarah's Egyptian maid, was allowed to have a baby by Abraham when Sarah was thought to be barren and they were fearful that God's promise wouldn't be kept. This was an acceptable practice in those days. Ishmael was the son of Abraham and Hagar. (Genesis 16:1–16; 21:1–21)

Haran (hay' ruhn), a city north of Palestine that later became the capital city of Assyria, was home for a time to Terah and Abraham. Terah, Abraham's father, settled there after leaving Ur, the city of the Chaldeans (later Babylonia) and the birthplace of Abraham. (Genesis 11:31; 12:4–5)

Isaac (eye' zuhk), son of Abraham and Sarah, was given his name because of his mother's response to God's promise. His name means "he laughs." As the heir of God's promise, Isaac's major renown came from being the son of Abraham and the father of Jacob. (Genesis 21:1–7; 24:1 to 28:9)

Ishmael (ish' may uhl), whose name means "God hears," was the son of Abraham and Hagar. After the birth of Isaac, the son of Abraham and Sarah, Ishmael and his mother Hagar were sent away. Ishmael married an Egyptian, had twelve sons who became princes and a daughter who became the wife of Esau! (Genesis 16:1–16; 21:1–21)

Israel. Context is important in understanding the use of the word "Israel." Israel was the new name given to Jacob after he wrestled with the angel at the Jabbok River. The name literally means "he who struggles with God." (Genesis 32:28) The name Israel was later given to all of the people of the covenant, and the promised land became known as the Land of Israel. After the division of Solomon's kingdom into Israel and Judah in the 10th century B.C., however, the term referred only to the Northern Kingdom.

Jacob, son of Isaac and Rebecca and twin of Esau, was given a name which could mean "he grabs the heel" or "he supplants." Jacob tricked his brother Esau twice to gain both the family birthright and his father Isaac's blessing.

Reassurance of God's covenant promises came to him in a vision of a ladder linking heaven and earth with ascending and descending angels. God's blessings and a new name, "Israel," were given to Jacob after wrestling "until the breaking of the day" with an angel at the Jabbok River. The new name perhaps meant "he struggles with God." Jacob/Israel was the father of the twelve tribes of Israel: Reuben, Simeon, Levi, Judah, Issachar, Zebulun, Dan, Naphtali, Gad, Asher, Joseph, and Benjamin. In many later references the names Jacob and Israel refer to the nation. (Genesis 25:21–34; 27:1 to 47:31)

Joseph, who provides the crucial link between the time of Abraham, Isaac, and Jacob and the time of the Exodus from Egypt, was one of Jacob's twelve sons. Joseph was sold into slavery in Egypt by his jealous brothers (see the map of the Journey of Joseph); thrown into prison in Egypt on false charges; released and given a position of authority because of his ability to interpret dreams; and eventually provided a way for his brothers and father to escape famine in Canaan by having them settle in Egypt. (Genesis 37:1 to 50:26)

Leah, Jacob's first wife, was not his favorite. Leah's father, Laban, tricked Jacob into marrying her, although he had been promised Leah's younger sister Rachel in exchange for seven years of service. Leah bore him six sons and a daughter. Her name means "cow," which indicates she was "cow-eyed." (Genesis 29:15–35)

Rachel, Jacob's favorite wife, bore him two sons, Joseph and Benjamin. She died during the birth of Benjamin. She and her sister Leah are considered two of the matriarchs (*mater* – Latin for mother) of Israel (Ruth 4:11). Rachel's name means "ewe." (Genesis 29:15–35)

Rebecca, daughter of Bethuel, was the wife of Isaac and mother of Jacob and Esau. She favored her younger son Jacob and assisted him in deceiving his father Isaac in order to receive his blessing. (Genesis 24:1–67; 25:19 to 28:5)

Sarah, whose original name was Sarai, was the wife of Abraham. Like Abram's, her name was changed as a sign of the covenant promise. "Sarai/Sarah" means "noble woman, princess." As had Abraham, Sarah received God's promise of a son in her old age with amusement and amazement. After she had permitted Abraham to have a child by her servant Hagar, God fulfilled the promise to Sarah and Abraham, and she gave birth to Isaac. (Genesis 11:29 to 12:5; 16:1 to 18:15)

Shechem, an important setting in the lives of Abraham, Jacob, and Joseph, was at one time considered the central city of Canaan. Now called Nablus, it is located 40 miles north of Jerusalem.

THE SEARCH BEGINS

By reading through the section above you have discovered that there are many people associated with *The Promise*. Make an effort to understand their relationships. If you have a Bible with sub-titles, build on them as you read these passages and make notes that will help you retell the story of *The Promise*. You may want to use these questions to guide your reading.

- *What promise did God make to Abraham, Isaac, and Jacob?*
- *How did this covenant change their lives?*
- *What significance for succeeding generations did God's promise have?*

Genesis 12:1–9, God's Promise to Abram (the map on page 40, "Journey of Abraham," shows where Abraham traveled)

Genesis 16:1–15, Hagar and Ishmael

Genesis 17:1–27, God's Covenant with Abraham

Genesis 18:1–15; 21:1–7, The Birth of Isaac

Genesis 21:9–21, Hagar and Ishmael Sent Away

Genesis 22:1–19, Abraham is Faithful

Genesis 25:19–34, The Birth of Jacob and Esau

Genesis 29:1–5, 13–30, Leah and Rachel

Genesis 32:22–32, Jacob Wrestles

Genesis 37:1–36, The Story of Joseph (the map on page 41, "Journey of Joseph," shows his travels)

Genesis 41:25–57; 42:1–5, Joseph Becomes Governor

Genesis 45:1–28, God Rescues Joseph's Family

Genesis 47:1–12, 27–31, Israel in Egypt

THE SEARCH CONTINUES

In these readings I have questions about...

In these readings I discovered...

FOCUSING THE SEARCH

As you pay close attention to the names and words in the biblical story, you will discover added insights. Abraham was the first of the patriarchs (from the Latin word *pater* which means father). In the Bible his name is translated "father of a multitude" in the *Revised Standard Version*. God's covenant promise that Abraham would have many descendants is reflected in his name. We often gain a better understanding of a person or a place or term in the Old Testament by knowing the meaning of the original Hebrew words. Because they are so important to our knowledge of the Bible, these meanings are often included in footnotes.

In the following exercise locate the passages in parentheses after each word. Using the footnotes in your Bible, write the way the word is rendered in the translation you are using.

Word in Hebrew	Word in English	Name/Word Means
יִשְׁמָעֵאל	Ishmael (Gen. 16:11)	_____
אַבְרָהָם	Abraham (Gen. 17:5)	ancestor of a multitude
	Isaac (Gen. 17:18; 18:9–15)	_____
עֵשָׂו	Esau (Gen. 25:30)	_____
יַעֲקֹב	Jacob (Gen. 25:26)	_____
אֱדוֹם	Edom (Gen. 25:30)	_____
בֵּית־אֵל	Bethel (Gen. 28:19)	_____
יוֹסֵף	Joseph (Gen. 30:23–24)	_____
יִשְׂרָאֵל	Israel (Gen. 32:28)	_____

There are many other interesting footnotes to the book of Genesis. Not all have to do with names. Footnotes enrich our understanding of the text. You will be wise to make reading them a habit.

PUTTING IT TOGETHER

Your family tree may be made up of brothers and sisters as well as parents, grandparents, aunts, uncles, cousins, and so on. Joseph, the last of the patriarchs, was part of a large and distinguished family. The exercise on page 42, "Joseph's Family Tree," will help you gain a better understanding of his ancestors and their relationships. This will also help you sort out the various stories from Abraham to Joseph (Genesis 12–50). Refer to your notes or "Preparing for the Search," if you are uncertain about how some of these people are related.

REFLECTION

1. God's renewal of the covenant with Abraham, Isaac, Jacob, and Joseph sets the tone for all that follows in the Bible. Throughout the stories we have read thus far, one fact stands out. God is faithful, even when people are not.

   Reflect upon God's faithfulness. What does this tell you about God's relationship to you? What does it tell you about your relationship to God?

2. Review Joseph's words to his brothers: "And now do not be distressed, or angry with yourselves, because you sold me here: for God sent me before you to preserve life." (Genesis 45:5)

   Joseph believed all that had happened to him was God's plan to rescue his family from starvation in Canaan. By arranging for the people of Israel to survive in Egypt, God was faithful to the promise.

   Think of times in your life when you have identified God at work bringing something good out of something that seemed bad. What have you discovered through that experience?

Journey of Abraham

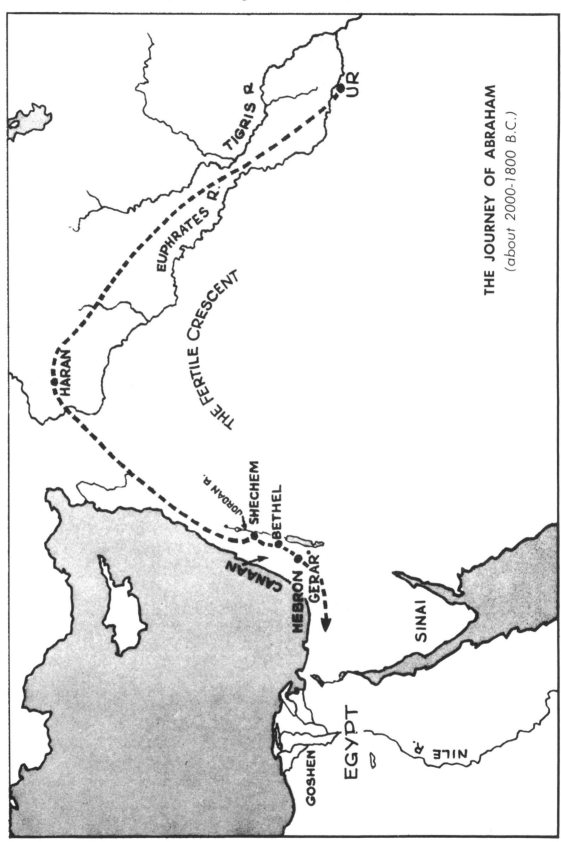

THE JOURNEY OF ABRAHAM
(about 2000-1800 B.C.)

Journey of Joseph

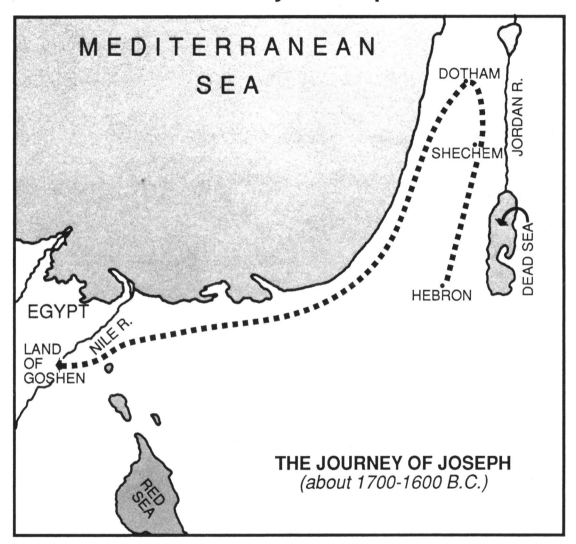

THE JOURNEY OF JOSEPH
(about 1700-1600 B.C.)

JOSEPH'S FAMILY TREE

Fill in the missing individuals on Joseph's family tree to help put together the various stories from Abraham to Joseph, Genesis 12–50

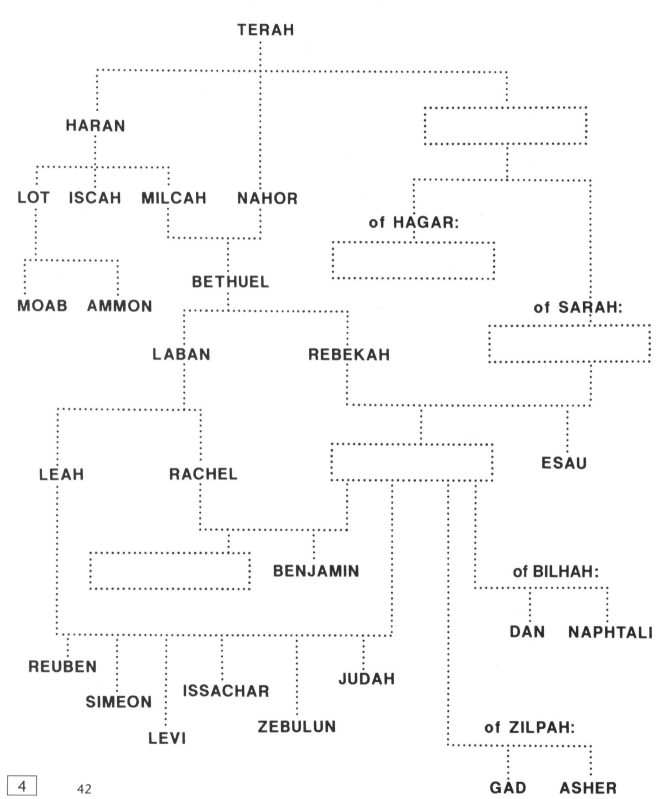

TERAH

HARAN

LOT   ISCAH   MILCAH   NAHOR

of HAGAR:

MOAB   AMMON

BETHUEL

of SARAH:

LABAN   REBEKAH

LEAH   RACHEL

ESAU

BENJAMIN

of BILHAH:

DAN   NAPHTALI

REUBEN

SIMEON   ISSACHAR   JUDAH

LEVI   ZEBULUN

of ZILPAH:

GAD   ASHER

The symbol for *The Exodus* is a burning flame set against the pyramids. God spoke to Moses from the burning bush.
(Exodus 3:2)

The Exodus

THE STORY CONTINUES

But Moses said to God, "If I come to the Israelites and say to them, 'The God of your ancestors has sent me to you,' and they ask me, 'What is his name?' what shall I say to them?"
Exodus 3:13

What has happened? As the book of *Genesis* ends, the descendants of Abraham, having been rescued from famine in Canaan, are living in Egypt. Yet, as the book of *Exodus* begins, they are the oppressed slaves of the Pharaoh. How will God's promise be fulfilled now?

God remembers the promise. Speaking from a burning bush, God calls Moses to confront Pharaoh and announce that God will lead the Israelites out of Egypt. But Moses questions God's call: Who am I to do this? What if they don't believe me? Who are you? God answers Moses' questions: I am with you, I will be with you, you will know me by what I do. Through a series of miraculous plagues, culminating in the death of Egypt's firstborn males, God acts to fulfill the promise made to Abraham, Isaac, and Jacob. God rescues the Israelites from slavery in Egypt and sets them free for their journey to the Promised Land.

In the Exodus from Egypt the Israelites come to know the name of God, Yahweh, but more importantly, they come to know the nature of God. In experiencing God's mighty deliverance, the Israelites will forever know God as one who promises and fulfills, calls and guides, rescues and protects. The experience of the Exodus is central to the faith of Israel, enlightening all that has happened from the beginning and influencing all that will follow.

PREPARING FOR THE SEARCH

Read about these key people, events, and places in *The Exodus* to prepare for your review of the Scripture passages.

Aaron, Moses' older brother, became the spokesman for Moses upon the direction of God. As leader *in absentia* when Moses was on Mount Sinai, it was Aaron who gave in to the people's demand to make a golden calf. Under God's instructions to Moses, Aaron and his sons were anointed to the office of priest. (Exodus 4:14–17; 5:1 to 12:51)

Angel, from the Greek word "angelos," means "a messenger." Angels of God were sent to Abraham, Hagar, Moses, Joshua, Elijah, Daniel, Jesus, Peter, and Paul, in addition to countless others. Angels are heavenly beings who serve God in heaven and on earth. (Exodus 3:2; 14:19)

Exodus, the second book of the Bible, is entitled "These are the names" in Hebrew. When the book was translated into Greek, the Greek word for departure (exodus) was substituted to refer to the central story in the book, Israel's dramatic exodus from Egypt.

Miriam, the sister of Moses and Aaron, is remembered both for her song of triumph after Israel crossed the Red Sea and as one who shared the leadership of the Hebrew people with her brothers. However, as a result of her words against Moses, she was stricken with leprosy. Moses interceded with God and she was healed. (Exodus 2:4, 7–8; 15:20–21; see also Numbers 12)

Moses, God's spokesman, leader, and statesman, could be considered the most important person in the Old Testament. Born a Hebrew yet raised an Egyptian, Moses led the Hebrew people out of Egyptian captivity at God's command. His leadership was crucial during the years in the wilderness when he helped form the new nation upon a powerful new understanding of God. (Exodus 2:1 to Deuteronomy 34:12)

Mount Sinai, or Mt. Horeb. The exact location is uncertain, but it is a mountain in the Sinai Peninsula where the Israelites camped following their exodus from Egypt. Three months after their arrival at Mount Sinai, God gave Moses the Ten Commandments. Today a traditional site of Mount Sinai is called Jebel Musa (Mountain of Moses). (Exodus 19:1 to 33:1)

Passover was the final event in God's deliverance of the Israelites from Egypt. God killed the first born children of the Egyptians but spared the first born of the Israelites, where blood had been sprinkled over the family doorways. The Passover meal, with ingredients symbolic of the entire Exodus event, celebrates God's saving act in the Passover. (Exodus 12:1–30)

BCE	c. 1900		1250	1210
	Patriarchs Abraham Isaac Jacob Joseph		**the Exodus** Moses Aaron Miriam	**the Conquest and Settlement** Joshua the Judges Samuel

5 44

Red Sea. The body of water that Israel crossed during the exodus from Egypt is more precisely translated "sea of reeds," the exact meaning of the Hebrew words. (Exodus 13:18 to 14:31)

THE SEARCH BEGINS

Begin your search by reading the following passages in your Bible. Make notes that will help you retell the story during the session. Use these questions to guide your readings.

- *What happened in the Exodus?*
- *Who were the major leaders during this time?*
- *Why do you think the Exodus is one of the most important events in the Old Testament?*

Exodus 3:1–20, God Calls Moses

Exodus 4:1–17, Moses is Given Power

1030	930		722/721	587/586	538		333		63
Monarchy Founded	**Divided Kingdom**	Elisha	**Fall of Samaria**	**Fall of Jerusalem**	**Return and Restoration**		**Greek Rule** Daniel		**Roman Rule**
Saul	Jeroboam	Jehu	Josiah	**Exile in**	Haggai		written		
David	Rehoboam	Amos	Zephaniah	**Babylon**	Zechariah				
Solomon	Ahab	Hosea		Ezekiel	Ezra				
	Elijah	Micah			Nehemiah				
		1 Isaiah							

Exodus 5:22–6:13, God's Plan

Exodus 12:1–36, The Passover

Exodus 12:37–42; 13:17–22, The Departure from Egypt

Exodus 14:1–31, Crossing the Red Sea

Exodus 15:1–21, Song of Liberation

Exodus 19:1–8, Camped at Mount Sinai

THE SEARCH CONTINUES

In these readings I have questions about...

In these readings I discovered...

FOCUSING THE SEARCH

In this discovery, as in the previous one, our focus is on the importance of names. Today, at least in our culture, names do not hold the same power they did in ancient times. When Moses asked for God's "name," he was not expressing idle curiosity. He was not even trying to make certain that the God who was confronting him in the burning bush was the God of his ancestors. Moses believed that he would have some control if he could call God by name.

In Exodus 3:14 the name God reveals to Moses is translated in the *Revised Standard Version* as I AM WHO I AM. The footnotes at the bottom of the page indicate that this same Hebrew word can be translated I AM WHAT I AM or I WILL BE WHO I WILL BE. Check the footnotes in your Bible to see what they say about God's name. One source indicates that it should probably be rendered, I CAUSE TO BE WHAT COMES INTO EXISTENCE.

The Hebrew letters for God's name in Exodus 3:14 are YHWH. Because the four letters are consonants, we do not know how this name of God was pronounced in Old Testament times. It wasn't until the early Christian era that Jewish editors of the Hebrew Scriptures, known as Masoretes, added vowel "points" to Hebrew words. Using these vowels, YHWH is translated in English as Yahweh. Even today, however, out of reverence and tradition, YHWH is not pronounced aloud by pious Jews. They substitute "Adonai"(ad-oh-ni') meaning "Lord." When you read "LORD" in an English translation, the Hebrew word behind it most likely is "Yahweh."

The Old Testament writers used a number of different names for God. Before the time of Moses the name El was used. Later it was often combined with other words to form new words. Therefore the city named Beth-el means "house of God." Eli-ezer ("God is a helper") is Moses' second son (Exodus 18:4).

Exodus 6:2–3 is an interesting passage because in it you will find three different names for God. Read it and then, using the information in the footnote and the information above, write the two verses, substituting the appropriate names for God.

_____

_____

_____

_____

Now use your Bible to complete the chart below. If you can check more than one translation, see what you can discover about the way different editors translate the Hebrew names for God into English.

THE NAMES OF GOD

Bible Reference	English/ Hebrew	Bible Dictionary Definition	Your Bible's Translation
Genesis 1:1	Elohim (e-loh-heem')	God	_____
Genesis 14:19	El Elyon (el el-yon)	God Most High	_____
Genesis 21:33	El Olam (el o-lam)	Everlasting God	_____
Exodus 6:2	Yahweh (yah'-way)	I Am Who I Am	_____
Exodus 6:3	El Shaddai (el shad' i)	The Mountain One	_____

If you get interested in this subject, you can usually discover other names for God by checking the heading Names of God in a good Bible dictionary such as *Harper's Bible Dictionary*.

PUTTING IT TOGETHER

One good way to get a "feel" for a passage of Scripture is to picture it in your mind. The story of the Exodus is very dramatic. Select one of the passages listed below. Look for clues that indicate the time of day, people involved, geographical setting, and action taking place. Using your imagination, visualize the scene. Then, using your ideas, do one of the following:

> *a.* Sketch the scene as simply or as elaborately as you wish.

> *b.* Pretend you are a movie director. Write a script that includes information for the design of the set.

> *c.* Put yourself in the scene. Write a first person account of what you saw and heard.

d. Write a newspaper article for *The Wilderness Journal* about the event.

e. Create your own idea!

You may be asked to present what you have done when we share the summaries of the passages read for this session on *The Exodus.*

- *Exodus 3:1–6, God Calls Moses*
- *Exodus 13:17–22, God Leads*
- *Exodus 15:20–21, Miriam's Song*
- *Exodus 4:1–9, Signs from God*
- *Exodus 12:37–42, The Exodus*
- *Exodus 14:15–31, Crossing the Sea*

REFLECTION

1. Think about the feelings of those who left Egypt to cross the desert. Many were apprehensive about an unknown future. Others welcomed the chance to start a new life. In what ways do your feelings and concerns about the future compare with those of the ancient Israelites? How does this story about the Exodus give you hope?

2. Reflect upon the experiences of the Israelites who left Egypt knowing that God was directly guiding their departure.

What experience in your life has convinced you of God's direction or perhaps intervention, to guide you or someone you know? In what ways does your experience give you an insight into Israel's response to their rescue?

The symbol for *The Journey* is the tablets of the Ten Command-ments, God's gift to the Israelites on Mount Sinai. (Exodus 24:12)

The Journey

THE STORY CONTINUES

"Why is the LORD bringing us into this land to fall by the sword? Our wives and our little ones will become booty; would it not be better for us to go back to Egypt?" Numbers 14:3

The departure from Egypt is hurried and dramatic: a passage through the sea, the destruction of Pharaoh's army, a guiding cloud by day, a pillar of fire by night, food in the desert, and water from a rock. Yet, soon the journey slows down. Unexpected hardships along the route bring angry complaints, and unanticipated delays bring challenging questions. All too soon the journey stops.

For forty years the Israelites live as nomads in the desert, waiting for God's command to enter Canaan, the land of promise. Rather than wandering aimlessly around the desert, most of their time is spent in the area of Kadesh-barnea, following an extended stay at Mount Sinai.

At Mount Sinai, God's covenant gift of the Ten Commandments confirms the ancient covenants made with Abraham, Isaac, and Jacob. During the stay at Sinai and Kadesh-barnea, God's Law expressed in the commandments is given further interpretation; the full implications of the covenant are closely linked with daily living. In addition, a strong, cohesive community is formed by linking together a leader gifted by God to lead a people called by God.

Why is God's promise of a homeland delayed? Some Israelites believe it is because of their lack of faith in God, as shown by their complaining and questioning. Others say that the assembled tribes need this extended time to organize and gain strength for the battles sure to come when occupied Canaan is entered. Whatever the reason for the delay, the wilderness stay is a critical time for Israel's future. Throughout the period, one question remains on their minds: "Is it the time yet, O Lord?"

PREPARING FOR THE SEARCH

Here are some words you will need to know as you begin your study of *The Journey*.

Ark of the Covenant, translated "the Covenant Box" in the *Good News Bible,* was a chest which held the stone tablets – the commandments. As a symbol representing Yahweh's presence with the people, the ark was carried into battle, led the procession when the people crossed the Jordan, and was ultimately placed in the Holy of Holies in Solomon's Temple in Jerusalem. The Ark of the Covenant disappeared in 586 B.C. when Jerusalem fell to Nebuchadnezzar. (Exodus 25:10–22; Numbers 10:33,35; Deuteronomy 10:1–5)

Caleb (kay' leb), one of the twelve spies sent into Canaan, joined Joshua in opposing those spies who said the Canaanites were too strong for the Israelites to conquer. Before the conquest Caleb helped determine the distribution of the land to the tribes and after the conquest was given the town of Hebron because of his trust in Yahweh's promises. (Numbers 13:1 to 14:45)

Deuteronomy, the fifth book of the Bible, part of the Torah or Pentateuch, is in the form of a speech by Moses as the Israelites are preparing to cross the Jordan River into Canaan. One of the most significant books in the Old Testament, Deuteronomy is one of the most quoted books in the New Testament, especially by Jesus. With its emphasis on personal obedience to God's will, this book guided the reform of the nation led by Josiah in 621 B.C.

Eleazar (el-ee-ay' zer), third surviving son of Aaron, became a priest when Aaron died. Aaron, who was in charge of the Levites under the leadership of both Moses and Joshua, helped distribute the land of Canaan to the twelve tribes. (Numbers 27:12–23)

Joshua, the son of Nun of the tribe of Ephraim, was Moses' successor as leader of the people during the entry into Canaan and the conquest of the land. As leader he demonstrated great military skill and complete loyalty to God. Joshua's name means "God is salvation." In the development from the Hebrew – "Joshua, Jehoshua, Jeshua" – to its translation in the Greek, the name became "Jesus." The meaning, of course, remained the same – "God is salvation." (Exodus 17:9–14; Numbers 14:6–30)

BCE	c. 1900		1250	1210
	Patriarchs Abraham Isaac Jacob Joseph		**the Exodus** Moses Aaron Miriam	**the Conquest and Settlement** Joshua the Judges Samuel

6   52

Manna, a word which means, "What is it?" (Exodus 16:15) or "gift" (Arabic), was the food given to the Israelites to sustain them during their 40 years in the wilderness. God stopped providing manna when the Hebrews crossed the Jordan to enter into Canaan. (Exodus 16:14–35)

Numbers, the fourth book in the Bible, is called "In the wilderness" in Hebrew. The Greek title, Numbers, was probably given because of the census at the beginning (Numbers 1:2) of the book. Numbers records the wilderness preparations made in advance of entering Canaan.

Shema (shuh-mah'), in Hebrew means "hear," and is the name of Israel's statement of faith in Deuteronomy 6:4–5: "Hear, O Israel: The Lord our God, the Lord is one. Love the Lord your God with all your heart and with all your soul and with all your strength."

Tent of Meeting. The tent of meeting was a movable sanctuary where God met with the people during the time of *The Journey.* It may also have been the place where Moses judged the people. There is some uncertainty about when this tent became the more formal Tabernacle described in Exodus 25 and following.

Ten Commandments, also called the "Decalogue" from the Greek for "ten words," express the essential laws needed for the life of the Hebrew community. The Ten Commandments, since their format encourages memorization, most likely were recited during ceremonies to renew the people's covenant with God.

Urim and Thummim (oo' reem, thoo' meem), one or more objects – what they actually were is uncertain – placed on the ephod, the vest of the priest, that were used to determine the will of God. The words, which translate "lights and perfections," begin with the first and last letters of the Hebrew alphabet. (Exodus 28:30; Numbers 27:21)

THE SEARCH BEGINS

The Journey lasted forty years. Much happened during that time. As you read the representative passages in this section, attempt to see the "big picture" rather than focusing on small details. Make careful notes about each selection so you will be able to retell the story. These questions may help you.

- *What happened on the journey through the wilderness?*
- *Why were the Israelites there so long?*
- *What important event happened on Mt. Sinai?*
- *What seems to be the major significance of the years of journeying?*

1030	930		722/721	587/586	538	333	63
Monarchy Founded	**Divided Kingdom**	Elisha	**Fall of Samaria**	**Fall of Jerusalem**	**Return and Restoration**	**Greek Rule**	**Roman Rule**
Saul	Jeroboam	Jehu	Josiah	**Exile in**	Haggai	Daniel	
David	Rehoboam	Amos	Zephaniah	**Babylon**	Zechariah	written	
Solomon	Ahab	Hosea		Ezekiel	Ezra		
	Elijah	Micah			Nehemiah		
		1 Isaiah					

Exodus 20:1–17, The Ten Commandments

Exodus 32:1–19, The Golden Calf

Exodus 34:1–10, The Second Tablets

Numbers 10:11–13, 29–36, The Journey Begins

Numbers 11:4–35, The People Complain

Numbers 13:1–2, 17–33, The Spies Enter Canaan

Numbers 20:1–13, God Provides Water

Numbers 27:12–23, Joshua Succeeds Moses

Deuteronomy 6:1–9, The Great Commandment

Deuteronomy 6:10–25, Remember Your Past

THE SEARCH CONTINUES

In these readings I have questions about...

In these readings I discovered...

FOCUSING THE SEARCH

In Discoveries 4 and 5 you practiced using your Bible's footnotes. As you worked with the footnotes, you noticed other notations that included Bible references, either at the bottom of the page, between the columns, or in the case of *Today's English Version*, sometimes under a chapter heading. These are called cross reference notes. They help you to locate other places in the Bible where a specific verse or passage is alluded to, repeated, or restated. Study Bibles usually have the most comprehensive cross reference notes. However, most Bibles include cross references for the more significant passages. Exodus 20:2–17 is such a passage.

Open your Bible to that passage. Locate the cross reference notes by finding the notation 20:2–17 or just 2–17 under a heading that says Ch. 20. Next to that you will find the other place in the Old Testament where the Ten Commandments are written. Write the reference here:

_____

Deuteronomy 6:4–5 is used by Jesus to answer the question, "...which is the greatest commandment in the law?" Using the cross reference notes, locate three places in the New Testament where Jesus quotes Deuteronomy 6:4–5.

1. _____   2. _____   3. _____

PUTTING IT TOGETHER

An awareness of the lands of the Bible is crucial for an understanding of the message of the Bible, because the Bible tells the story of a people linked to a specific time and place, bound to particular settings and locations, influenced by geography and climate. Therefore, it is often helpful to consult a map when you read a story in the Bible. This is especially true when travel, distances, and geography are key parts of that story. Knowing the distance involved in the story of *The Journey* can influence the ways one understands this part of the story. Turn to the map of "Egypt And Sinai", which will be found on page 59 at the end of this discovery.

- *Locate Mt. Sinai, Wilderness of Sin (or Zin), Wilderness of Paran, Kadesh Barnea (or Kadesh), Canaan.*
- *Figure these distances: Bitter Lakes to Mt. Sinai; Mt. Sinai to Kadesh Barnea; Kadesh Barnea to Hebron in Canaan.*

Since it happened over 3000 years ago, it should not surprise you to learn that no one knows the exact route taken by the Israelites. Those who wrote the account of *The Journey* were not interested in providing us with a detailed and precise itinerary. They were more interested in telling us about the great things God had done for the people. However, if you are interested in learning more about the possible route taken, look at a map of The Exodus in a Bible atlas. That map will not only include the traditional route, but may also indicate one or more other routes some scholars believe to be feasible.

REFLECTION

1. Reflect upon the reactions of those who made the journey from Egypt. What are some of the emotions the Israelites may have been experiencing during their journey to the promised land?

   What seemed to be the main causes of the grumbling and complaining by the people? What similarities do you see between then and now?

2. Think about the leadership qualities exhibited by Caleb and Joshua. Who are some men and women today who exhibit some of these same leadership qualities? Which of these qualities do you see in yourself? How might God be calling you to use them?

Egypt and Sinai

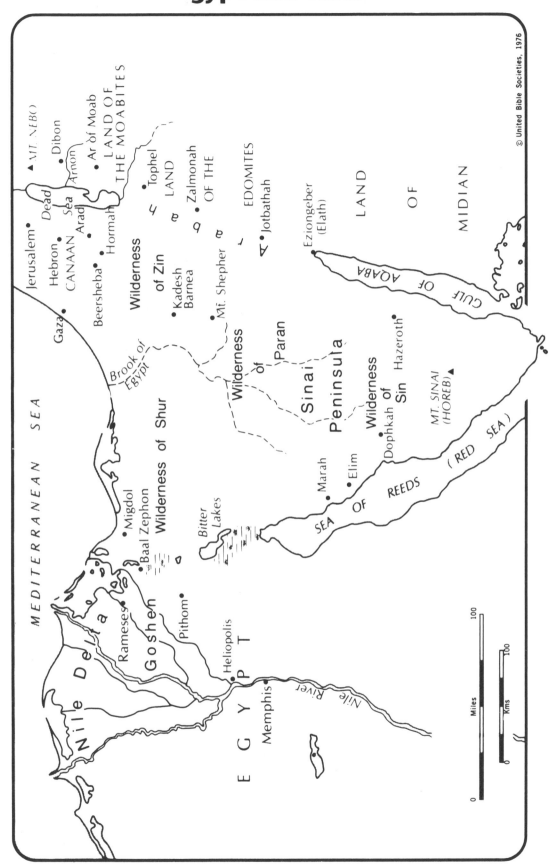

© United Bible Societies, 1976

59

6

The symbol for *The Conquest* is a Shofar, a ram's horn which represents the horns blown at the battle of Jericho. (Joshua 6:4)

The Conquest

THE STORY CONTINUES

Gideon answered him, "But sir, if the LORD is with us, why then has all this happened to us? And where are all his wonderful deeds that our ancestors recounted to us, saying, 'Did not the LORD bring us up from Egypt?'" Judges 6:13

God has not forgotten! After forty years the Israelites are ready; the training and preparations have been made! At God's command, Joshua and the people cross over the Jordan River from the East to begin the conquest of Canaan, God's promised land. Yet, the conquest of a land already held by the Canaanites, Amorites, Girgashites, Hittites, Perizzites, Hivites, and Jebusites is to take over 250 years.

Joshua leads the first stages of the conquest. After initial victories at Jericho, Ai, Shechem, and Hazor, however, the struggle turns into an extended conflict. The Canaanites, who already inhabit the area, do not agree that Yahweh, the God of the Israelites, has claimed their land. The Canaanite gods, Baal and Asherah, do not confirm this at all. In fact, for the Canaanites the land is no more Joshua's than it once was Abraham's, Isaac's, or Jacob's. On the other hand, the Israelites see the conquest of Canaan not only as a crucial and inevitable part of their covenant with God (Yahweh), but also as God's judgment on the sins of the Canaanites. Centuries later, when Israel is itself invaded and conquered, the prophets view defeat through the same eyes of faith; it is God's judgment on Israel's sins.

Following Joshua's death, the warfare and settlement of the land is carried on by the inspired leadership of judges, such as Deborah, Gideon, and

Samson. These judges function as clan leaders who occasionally rally the forces of many clans against an enemy, rather than as judges in the modern sense. When the initial conquest is over, the land of Canaan is divided up among the twelve tribes of Israel in the hope that each tribe will secure its boundaries and maintain its hold on the land.

Yet, when warfare ceases and the Israelites settle in to farm the land, they themselves are tempted to worship the fertility gods of the Canaanites rather than remain faithful to Yahweh, the God of the Covenant. Surviving in the promised land demands more than inspired leadership.

PREPARING FOR THE SEARCH

These words will help you as you prepare to study *The Conquest.*

Astarte (ah-stahr'te), also known as Asherah (ah'sher-ah) or Ashtoreth, was a Canaanite fertility goddess. She and Baal (see below) were consorts. The word Asherah also refers to a wooden pole that was placed in Canaanite places of worship as a symbol of the deity.

Baal (bay'al) is the name for the supernatural beings responsible for fertility in the Canaanite religion. By the time the Hebrews entered the land it was also the proper name for the most important deity of the Canaanites. Baal is frequently associated with the goddess Asherah. By the time of Elijah, during the reign of Ahab and Jezebel, the worship of Baal had almost supplanted that of Yahweh. Elijah's staged contest on Mount Carmel between Baal and Yahweh resulted in the slaughter of the priests of Baal. Much of the Old Testament, especially 1 and 2 Kings, is devoted to the intense struggle between the worship of Yahweh and the worship of Baal. (Judges 2:11, 13; 1 Samuel 7:4)

Dagon was the national god of the Philistines. He was thought to be responsible for the grain harvest. (Judges 16:23)

Deborah, a prophet and judge during the time of the conquest, was able to gather an immense army with the help of the Israelite BARAK and defeat SISERA, a powerful Canaanite enemy. Deborah's song of triumph in battle is one of the oldest Hebrew poems in the Bible. (Judges 4:1 to 5:31)

Eli, high priest at the sanctuary in Shiloh and a judge, was the one who trained the young Samuel in his priestly duties. Eli's two sons, Hophni and Phineas, did not maintain behavior appropriate for priests and, as a result,

BCE	c. 1900		1250	1210
	Patriarchs		**the**	**the**
	Abraham		**Exodus**	**Conquest**
	Isaac		Moses	**and**
	Jacob		Aaron	**Settlement**
	Joseph		Miriam	Joshua
				the Judges
				Samuel

were killed in a battle with the Philistines in which the Ark of the Covenant was captured. (1 Samuel 1:1 to 4:18)

Gideon, another of the judges, is known for his destruction of an altar to Baal and a highly successful night attack on the Midianites. (The complete story of Gideon is found in Judges 6:1 through 8:32.)

Jericho is the site of the oldest settlement in Palestine and is regarded by some as the oldest city in the world. It was the site of many crucial scenes in Israel's history. It is situated in the valley of the Jordan River, about five miles from the northern end of the Dead Sea and seventeen miles east of Jerusalem. Jericho was the site of Joshua's first triumph in the land of Canaan. (Joshua 5:13 to 6:27)

Judge is the title given to those special leaders God called at various times to rally the people, lead in battle, and maintain the tenuous peace during the period of the conquest of Canaan. A judge can best be understood as a clan leader, often with charismatic qualities, who of necessity gathered other tribes to meet a particular crisis. Some of the best known judges were Othniel, Deborah, Gideon, Jephthah, and Samson.

Philistines (fil' is-teens). These people occupied an area called Philistia, on Palestine's Southern Coast of the Mediterranean Sea. Called the "People of the Sea," they were also known for the manufacturing of iron tools and weapons. At the time of the Exodus the Hebrews went around Philistia to avoid conflict. The two nations remained enemies for centuries.

Rahab, a prostitute in Jericho, helped hide Joshua's spies when they entered the city. She then helped them to escape. She was received into the Hebrew community once Jericho had fallen, and she became the mother of Boaz. In this manner she became a member of Jesus' family tree. (Joshua 2:1–24; Joshua 6:25; Matthew 1:5)

Samson was one of the judges. He was dedicated to Yahweh as a Nazirite before he left his mother's womb. Being a Nazirite, he was forbidden to drink alcoholic beverages, cut the hair on his head, and go near dead bodies. Known for his incredible strength, and for the presence of the Spirit of the Lord, he was constantly engaged in fighting the Philistines. The entire saga of Samson is found in Judges 13:1 to 16:31.

Samuel, often called the last of the judges and the first of the great prophets, was dedicated to the priesthood at Shiloh by his parents, Elkanah and Hannah. Hannah's song at Samuel's birth (1 Samuel 2:1ff) serves as prelude to Mary's song about Jesus' birth in Luke 1:40ff. At first Samuel opposed the monarchy, but then went along with it, anointing both Saul and David

1030	930		722/721	587586	538	333	63
Monarchy Founded	**Divided Kingdom**	Elisha	**Fall of Samaria**	**Fall of Jerusalem**	**Return and Restoration**	**Greek Rule**	**Roman Rule**
Saul	Jeroboam	Jehu	Josiah	**Exile in**	Haggai	Daniel	
David	Rehoboam	Amos	Zephaniah	**Babylon**	Zechariah	written	
Solomon	Ahab	Hosea		Ezekiel	Ezra		
	Elijah	Micah			Nehemiah		
		1 Isaiah					

to the throne of Israel. Even so, he remained a critic of the king and was a powerful force in the royal court. (1 Samuel 1:1 to 4:22; 1 Samuel 7:3 to 16:13)

Shechem was the first worship center of the tribes of Israel. It was here that Joshua and the tribal leaders renewed the covenant they first entered into during *The Journey.* (Joshua 24:1–26)

THE SEARCH BEGINS

Read the passages listed below. As you read, make notes that will help you to retell the story of *The Conquest.* In each passage (except Judges 2:6 – 3:6) you will encounter someone with leadership ability. After your notes write the name of a person you identify as a leader and an adjective that describes a characteristic of the leader.

Think about these questions as you read.

- *How did contact with the Canaanite religion cause problems for the Israelites?*
- *In what ways was The Conquest more difficult than The Journey ?*

Joshua 1:1–18, Cross the Jordan!

Joshua 6:1–27, The Battle of Jericho

Joshua 24:1–28, The Shechem Covenant

Judges 2:6–23, Israel Forgets God

Judges 4:1–24, Deborah and Barak

Judges 6:1–40, Gideon and the Altar of Baal

Judges 13:1–5; 16:4–31, Samson and Delilah

1 Samuel 3:1–21, Samuel the Prophet

1 Samuel 7:3–17, Samuel Rules Israel

THE SEARCH CONTINUES

In these readings I have questions about...

In these readings I discovered...

FOCUSING THE SEARCH

The Psalms often recount the history of Israel. Several psalms proclaim God's mighty acts from the time of *The Covenant* to *The Conquest* of Canaan. Two, Psalms 105 and 106, describe a long span in Israel's history. They can serve as a mid-point review for the Old Testament portion of this course.

Read Psalm 105 and Psalm 106 and indicate the verses that summarize *The Promise, The Exodus, The Journey,* and *The Conquest.*

	Psalm 105	**Psalm 106**
The Covenant	_____	_____
The Exodus	_____	_____
The Journey	_____	_____
The Conquest	_____	_____

Try your hand at writing some new verses proclaiming the virtues of one or more of the Judges. After all, Samuel is the only one of the Judges mentioned in any of the psalms. (Psalm 99:6)

PUTTING IT TOGETHER

Not only is it important to keep a map in mind when we read the Bible, but also to picture the landscape, vegetation, and even the climate. What can you discover about the land of Canaan from the following passages?

Numbers 13:17–29 _____

_____

Deuteronomy 11:8–12 _____

_____

Joshua 5:10–12 _____

_____

When the conquest was finally complete, the land was divided among the twelve tribes of Israel (Jacob). Although not all passages of Scripture that list the tribes agree, these are the divisions shown on the map "Division Of Canaan", which you will find on page 70: Asher, Naphtali, Zebulun, Issachar, Manasseh (east and west), Ephraim, Gad, Dan, Benjamin, Reuben, Judah, and Simeon. The tribe of Levi, comprised of priests, was not given land.

Use the map to locate these cities associated with leaders in *The Conquest*. On the line next to the city write the name of the tribal territory in which it is located.

Leader	City	Tribe
Joshua	Jericho	_____
Deborah	Bethel	_____
Joshua	Shechem	_____
Deborah	Mount Tabor	_____
Samson	Gaza	_____
Samuel	Shiloh	_____

REFLECTION

1. What are your thoughts and feelings about the conquest of Canaan? Many people, perhaps because of the brutality and bloodshed, want to differentiate between God in the Old Testament and God in the New Testament. How does your understanding of God influence your understanding of the conquest of the land, and vice versa? In what ways do you think the conquest of the land influenced the way the ancient Israelites understood God?

2. Let the significance of Judges 2:10 sink in: "Moreover, that whole generation was gathered to their ancestors; and another generation grew up after them, who did not know the LORD or the work that he had done for Israel."

   What might happen to the church if ours was the last generation that remembered all that God has done?

Division of Canaan

7   70

The symbol for *The Kings* is a crown with three points, representing Saul, David, and Solomon, the three rulers of the United Kingdom.

The Kings

THE STORY CONTINUES

"Who is the King of glory? The LORD, strong and mighty, the LORD, mighty in battle." Psalm 24:8

From the time of *The Exodus*, God is the acknowledged ruler of the Israelites. However, toward the end of the time of *The Conquest*, the demand for an earthly king grows intense. Samuel's sons, neither strong nor of good character, are not able to carry on the leadership provided by their father. New leadership comes in the form of an earthly king. Even though Samuel reminds the people that Almighty God is their king and accurately predicts what it will mean to be ruled by a human monarch, the people still demand one, saying, "No! but we will have a king over us, that we also may be like all the nations, and that our king may govern us and go out before us and fight our battles." (1 Samuel 8:19b-20)

Guided by God, Samuel anoints Saul, from the tribe of Benjamin, and the monarchy begins. When the twelve tribes unite under a king, Israel is transformed. Saul, a victorious warrior, pulls the tribes together, yet his own inner turmoil tears him apart. David, whom Saul distrusts and tries to destroy, succeeds him when he and his son Jonathan are killed in battle. A poetic hero, David drives the Jebusites from Jerusalem and then triumphantly brings God's Ark of the Covenant into the city, making Jerusalem the political center of the nation. Because of this his dynasty is blessed forever. David's son Solomon rules the nation at its peak of wealth and influence, builds a magnificent temple for God, and yet ultimately weakens the foundation of the nation.

The reigns of Israel's first three kings make a tremendous impact upon the nation's political and religious life. The borders, which are extended farther than ever before or since, are secure. The arts flourish, literature is written, and the economy booms. Unfortunately, the days of the United Monarchy are brief; the cost of unity becomes burdensome. Solomon's reign ends with dissension among the people because of heavy taxation, foreign religious influences, and forced labor crews. Leadership which promotes faithfulness to God and obedience to God's covenant is desperately needed.

PREPARING FOR THE SEARCH

These people and places are important in the story of *The Kings.*

Bethlehem, before being honored as the birthplace of Jesus, was known as the home of Ruth, her grandson Jesse, and his son David. In Bethlehem, just five miles southwest of Jerusalem, Samuel anoints David, the future king of Israel. Eventually, the birthplace of King David becomes known as "the city of David."

David, son of Jesse and the second king of the United Kingdom of Israel, is probably the most popular figure in the Old Testament. Throughout the ages the Jews have revered King David in history and legend much as the English have idolized King Arthur. David's all-too-human traits are well documented in the Scriptures. In spite of his shortcomings his people loved him and readily forgave him. Because of God's everlasting covenant with him, David is the central and critical link in Jesus' family tree. (1 Samuel 16:1 to 1 Kings 2:11)

Hebron (hee'bruhn), a town in the hill country of Judah, was the capital city of David before he conquered Jerusalem. It was a city of refuge where people could claim safety from vengeance if they had accidentally killed someone. Abraham camped near Hebron; and from Hebron, King David's son, Absalom, led his rebellion. (Joshua 14:6–15; 2 Samuel 2:1–4)

Holy War. It was common among the nations of the Ancient Near East to look upon their warfare as a holy activity, sanctioned by their gods. In Israel such holy war was thought to be initiated by Yahweh, who alone was responsible for victory. The main task of the people was "mopping up" after the battle's outcome had been determined. Israel's military engagements were thus often viewed as power struggles between their God and the deities of other nations. The practice of totally destroying the enemy, which is mentioned in 1 Samuel 15, emphasizes the sacrificial nature of this warfare.

BCE	c. 1900		1250	1210
	Patriarchs Abraham Isaac Jacob Joseph		**the Exodus** Moses Aaron Miriam	**the Conquest and Settlement** Joshua the Judges Samuel

While the idea of making a whole people a sacrifice to Yahweh is repugnant to us, to disobey as Saul did, was considered an affront to God and a threat to the religious purity of the community.

Jeroboam I (jair-uh-boh'uhm), whose father was an official under King Solomon, was the first king of the Northern Kingdom of Israel. The prophet Ahijah, on meeting Jeroboam, tore his robe into twelve pieces to portray how Jeroboam would tear away ten of the tribes to form the new kingdom. Jeroboam's sin was the worship of idols: he set a golden calves in the sanctuaries of Bethel and Dan. (1 Kings 11:26 to 14:20)

Jerusalem, a city dating back to the third millennium B.C., was a stronghold of the Jebusites before David captured it around 1000 B.C. and made it the capital of the United Kingdom. It is strategically located on the central ridge of Palestine. David made Jerusalem the center of religious and political life for the united tribes. It became known as the city of David.

Jesse, grandson of Ruth and Boaz, was assured a place in history when he became the father of David. Jesus is a descendant of Jesse.

Nathan was a prophet in the court of King David and King Solomon. He told David that the temple he wished to build for God would be built instead by his son. Nathan also did not hesitate to proclaim God's word and call King David to task for his sinful affair with Bathsheba. He pronounced God's judgment by telling the famous parable of the poor man's ewe lamb. Nathan also played a critical role in bringing Solomon to the throne. (2 Samuel 7:1–17; 2 Samuel 12:1–25)

Saul, through the Spirit of the LORD, was anointed by Samuel as the first king of Israel. Saul experienced severe fits of depression and, after a reign of military successes and personal failures, toward the end of his career even consulted a fortuneteller, breaking one of his own laws. Saul was a tragic figure who began his reign with great promise, yet ended in shame and disaster. (1 Samuel 8:1 to 31:13)

Solomon, son of David and Bathsheba, was the third and last king of the United Kingdom. He actually had two names: "Solomon" which means "peace, welfare," and "Jedidiah" which translates "beloved of the Lord." Solomon created massive building programs (the Temple and the Palace), conscripted his own people for the labor force, married foreign wives who were allowed to observe their own religions, and generally lived like an oriental potentate. Solomon was known for his wisdom, and a number of proverbs are attributed to him.

Zion, one of the hills of Jerusalem, became the sacred "Mount Zion" after David captured Jerusalem from the Jebusites and renamed it "the city of David." King Solomon built the Temple on Mount Moriah, but both hills

1030	930		722/721	587/586	538	333	63
Monarchy Founded	**Divided Kingdom**	Elisha	**Fall of Samaria**	**Fall of Jerusalem**	**Return and Restoration**	**Greek Rule**	**Roman Rule**
Saul	Jeroboam	Jehu	Josiah	**Exile in**	Haggai	Daniel	
David	Rehoboam	Amos	Zephaniah	**Babylon**	Zechariah	written	
Solomon	Ahab	Hosea		Ezekiel	Ezra		
	Elijah	Micah			Nehemiah		
		1 Isaiah					

were referred to as Zion. In the Bible the word "Zion" often refers to God's people, as well as God's heavenly Jerusalem. (2 Samuel 5:7)

THE SEARCH BEGINS

The following passages will help you understand the people, events, and places associated with *The Kings*. Take careful notes so that you will be able to retell the story during the group session. As you read, focus on the "whole picture" by thinking about these questions:

- *What were some of the successes and failures of the kings?*
- *What changes took place in Israel because of the kings?*
- *What kind of leadership did each of the kings provide?*

1 Samuel 7:15–8:22, The People Want a King

1 Samuel 10:17–27, Saul is Chosen King

1 Samuel 15:10–35, Saul is Rejected

1 Samuel 17:12–54, David Kills Goliath

2 Samuel 5:1–12, David is Proclaimed King

2 Samuel 6:12–23, The Ark in Jerusalem

2 Samuel 7:1–17, God's Covenant with David

1 Kings 2:1–4,10–12, David's Death

1 Kings 3:1–15, Solomon's Prayer

1 Kings 6:1–14, Solomon Builds the Temple

1 Kings 11:1–13, Solomon Rejects God

1 Kings 11:26–40, God's Promise to Jeroboam

THE SEARCH CONTINUES

In these readings I have questions about...

In these readings I discovered...

FOCUSING THE SEARCH

In 1 Samuel 7:15–8:22 you read about the demand of the people for an earthly king "like all the nations." However, the kings of Israel were not like the kings of other nations. While other kings ruled with absolute power, the kings of Israel served only as long as they were obedient to God's commands.

Whenever God was angered by the actions of a king of Israel, a prophet pronounced the punishment to be accorded the one who had sinned. A particularly haunting story, illustrating this difference between the power of other kings and the kings of Israel, is told in 2 Samuel 11:1–12:15. King David becomes infatuated with Bathsheba, the wife of Uriah, one of his soldiers. When Bathsheba discovers she is pregnant, King David tries to trick Uriah into sleeping with her so that he will believe the child is his. However, Uriah is such an honorable man that he refuses to be with his wife as long as his fellow soldiers are in battle and suffering. When this ploy fails, King David has Uriah put at the front of a fierce battle so that he will be killed. Then he and Bathsheba marry.

Read 2 Samuel 12:1–15 to discover how God responds to David's treachery through the prophet Nathan. When you have finished reading, express your understanding of the relationship between a king of Israel and God using cinquain poetry. Cinquain is a simple, but effective type of poetry that follows this form:

line 1	Title – a noun	one word
line 2	Describes the title	two words
line 3	Action words about title	three words
line 4	Describes feelings about title	four words
line 5	Refers back to title	one word

Examples

King	David
God's chosen	Arrogant ruler
Rules the nation	Has Uriah killed
Must always obey Yahweh	He will be punished
David	Repentant

Write your poem(s) here.

PUTTING IT TOGETHER

The reason given for the rise of the monarchy in Israel is recorded in 1 Samuel 8:19b-20: "No! but we will have a king over us, that we also may be like all the nations, and that our king may govern us and go out before us and fight our battles."

The conquest of the Promised Land was still not completed, and the tribes needed to defend the territory they had already conquered. The power of the surrounding nations seemed to necessitate a strong army and a strong commander in charge. These other nations had kings. Therefore, a king of their own appeared to be a reasonable request from God's people.

In 1 Samuel 7:15–8:22 you read Samuel's warning about the problems associated with having a king. Of course, not everyone agreed with his reasoning. Now that you have had an opportunity to read the passages in "The Search Begins," you probably have your own opinion about the issue. List below at least five reasons *for* and five reasons *against* having a king.

Reasons for a king	Reasons against a king
_____	_____
_____	_____
_____	_____
_____	_____
_____	_____
_____	_____
_____	_____
_____	_____
_____	_____

REFLECTION

1. Reflect upon the concept of God as the ultimate "Ruler of Israel." Seeking military and political security, the people of Israel wanted an earthly king so that they could vie with other nations.

When are some times you have felt that you had to compromise to gain security or to compete? Where have you had to settle for less than the best? How have we, as a nation or people, attempted to protect our interests with various economic, political, or military "guarantees" today?

2. Reflect upon the significance of David's bringing the Ark of the Covenant into Jerusalem. From that time on, the glory of God was localized and a holy place was established. What do you think that meant, both good and bad, for the faith of Israel? In what ways do you see efforts made today to localize God and set up holy places? In what ways are you affected by these efforts?

The symbol for *The Two Kingdoms* is two crowns, representing the division into the Northern and Southern Kingdoms. (1 Kings 12:20)

The Two Kingdoms

THE STORY CONTINUES

Elijah then came near to all the people, and said, "How long will you go limping with two different opinions? If the LORD is God, follow him; but if Baal, then follow him." 1 Kings 18:21

What has gone wrong? In 931 B.C., King Solomon's successor, his son Rehoboam, faces a rebellion from the northern tribes led by Jeroboam. Jeroboam's revolt divides the United Kingdom of Israel into a Northern Kingdom of ten tribes, called Israel, and the Southern Kingdom of two tribes, called Judah. The Northern Kingdom, centered in Shechem, exists for 209 years until it is conquered by the Assyrians in 721 B.C. During that time it is ruled by nineteen kings. The Southern Kingdom of Judah, centered in Jerusalem and ruled by twenty monarchs, exists for 344 years until it is conquered by the Babylonians in 586 B.C.

The extensive story of the two kingdoms, recorded in 1 and 2 Kings (and in 1 and 2 Chronicles), is confusing, interwoven, and difficult to follow. Not only do the kings' reigns overlap, but some share the same name! At times the two kingdoms unite to fight a common enemy, but most of the time they battle each other. In this Discovery our attention will center on several kings and the prophets Elijah and Elisha.

To understand this period in the history of Israel and Judah, it is important to focus on the big picture rather than the details. The big picture is the continuing struggle of rulers and people to remain faithful and obedient to God in the face of rival gods and tempting beliefs. Elijah's question to the Israelites sums it up: " How long will you go limping with two different opinions?"

There are distinct differences between the two kingdoms. Judah's kings are descendants of David, whereas Israel's kings gain the crown through revolt and power struggles. The Southern Kingdom, due to the Temple in Jerusalem, seems less subject to foreign religious influences than is the Northern Kingdom, which has no one religious center. When the armies of the Assyrians and Babylonians invade and conquer, the people of Israel and Judah become captives once again; many are transported to foreign lands. What has gone wrong?

PREPARING FOR THE SEARCH

The people and places described below play a significant role in the story of *The Two Kingdoms*.

Ahab, king of Israel for twenty-two years, was the son of Omri, the ruler who founded an important dynasty and moved the capital to Samaria. Ahab married Jezebel, a woman from Sidon who was a follower of the god Baal. A weak leader, he built an altar for his wife's god and vacillated in his own faith. During his reign Baalism grew in power and appeal. For this reason, he was constantly in conflict with Elijah whom he called the "troubler of Israel." (1 Kings 16:29–34; 1 Kings 18:1–46)

Anointing in the Bible is an act with many meanings. It may refer to an act of hospitality in which oil is placed upon the head to welcome a guest. Anointing was also customary for medicinal and surgical purposes. In addition, anointing may indicate the official setting apart of a prophet, priest, or king for holy duties. In this sense anointing refers to God's setting apart a unique individual to be the Messiah (Christ), whose title translates as "the anointed one."

Assyria/Babylonia. These are the names of two ancient nations located in the regions of the Tigris and Euphrates rivers. Assyria is a rich plain in the northern part of the region with its capital at Assur. Babylonia, also called Chaldea, runs south to the Persian Gulf, with its capital at Babylon. Both nations had a long history prior to their military encounters with Israel and Judah, and their literature and religion are thought to have influenced several of the stories in Genesis 1–11. In 721 B.C. the Assyrians under Shalmaneser captured Samaria and defeated the Northern Kingdom. Jerusalem and Judah fell to Nebuchadnezzar, the Babylonian ruler, in 586 B.C.

Elijah (ee-li'juh), a native of Tishbe in Galilee, is usually considered to be the first of the prophets. He spent much of his life in mortal battle with Baalism, the Canaanite fertility religion. His major enemies were King Ahab

BCE	c. 1900		1250	1210
	Patriarchs Abraham Isaac Jacob Joseph		**the Exodus** Moses Aaron Miriam	**the Conquest and Settlement** Joshua the Judges Samuel

and Ahab's wife, Jezebel. Elijah understood that a central part of his work as a prophet was to call the king to task when he strayed from righteousness and true worship. Since Ahab's wife, Jezebel, was a notorious Baal worshiper, Elijah had a fertile field to plow. Elijah exhibited a characteristic common to great spiritual leaders: he grew and matured in his understanding of God and what God wanted him to be and do. Elijah also emphasized that social justice was an important ingredient of true religion. (1 Kings 17:1 to 2 Kings 2:11)

Elisha (ee-li'-shah), whose name means "El (God) is salvation," succeeded Elijah and received Elijah's prophetic mantle. For 50 years, through the reigns of six kings, he prophesied in Israel. Many of Elisha's experiences echo the miracles and teachings of Elijah. (1 Kings 19:16 to 2 Kings 13:21)

Hoshea (hoh-shee'uh) was the last king of Israel. His nine-year reign did not improve in quality, but even so he was judged better than those who had reigned previously! Hoshea's military alliance with Egypt and his withholding of tribute eventually brought about the wrath of Assyria. The Northern Kingdom fell when Samaria, its capital city, was conquered in 721 B.C. (2 Kings 17:1–6)

Israel, the Northern Kingdom. Upon the death of King Solomon the United Kingdom split in two. Jeroboam gathered ten tribes, with a territory three times the size of Judah (the Southern Kingdom) to form Israel, the Northern Kingdom. He established Shechem as the first capital of the kingdom (Samaria was later the capital), and set up golden calves in two shrines – Dan and Bethel. The history of the kingdom was tumultuous with 19 kings ruling over a 209 year period. Eight kings were killed or committed suicide, and seven reigned for less than two years.

Jehu (jay'hoo) became king of Israel in 843 B.C. following a bloody coup in which he killed King Jehoram. Elijah had been commanded by God to anoint him as ruler of the Northern Kingdom. However, the task was finally carried out by one of the "sons of the prophets" at the order of Elisha. Jehu ruled for twenty-eight years. During that time he carried out religious reforms and gained the support of the military, the prophets, and the general population. His dynasty lasted for ninety years. (2 Kings 9:1 to 10:36)

Jezebel, wife of King Ahab and fervent worshiper of the god Baal, used her considerable influence to persecute anyone and destroy anything associated with Yahweh, God of Israel. In the name of her foreign fertility religion she had prophets of Yahweh killed, their property confiscated, and then sought to kill Elijah, God's prophet. (1 Kings 16:31; 1 Kings 18:4,13)

1030	930		722/721	587/586	538	333	63
Monarchy Founded	**Divided Kingdom**	Elisha	**Fall of Samaria**	**Fall of Jerusalem Exile in Babylon**	**Return and Restoration**	**Greek Rule**	**Roman Rule**
Saul	Jeroboam	Jehu	Josiah	Ezekiel	Haggai	Daniel written	
David	Rehoboam	Amos	Zephaniah		Zechariah		
Solomon	Ahab	Hosea			Ezra		
	Elijah	Micah			Nehemiah		
		1 Isaiah					

Josiah (joh-si'uh), who became King of Judah at the age of eight, ruled for thirty-one years. In 621 B.C., during repairs to the Temple, the "book of the law," generally considered to be parts of Deuteronomy, was found by the High Priest Hilkiah and read to Josiah. As a result of hearing these words, Josiah led a sweeping religious reform of Judah which included a renewal of the covenant and a celebration of Passover. Josiah died in battle, fighting on the side of the Assyrians against the Egyptians. (2 Kings 21:24 to 23:30)

Judah, the Southern Kingdom. Two tribes, Judah and the greater part of Benjamin, were loyal to the line of David when the United Kingdom split following King Solomon's death. Nineteen kings and one queen ruled the Southern Kingdom for 344 years until Babylon conquered Jerusalem, the capital, in 586 B.C. The Southern Kingdom, though much smaller in territory, received many immigrants from the Northern Kingdom who were loyal to the throne of David and were horrified when Jeroboam set up the golden calves as idols in the shrines of Dan and Bethel.

Mount Carmel is a promontory that juts out above the Mediterranean Sea in central Palestine. It was an important location in the life of the prophet Elijah. It was on Mount Carmel that he challenged the priests of Baal and at a later time saw the cloud that formed over the Mediterranean Sea signaling the end of the drought. (1 Kings 18:19–20, 42–46)

Naaman, commander in the army of Ben-hadad, King of Syria, was sent to the King of Israel to be cured of leprosy. After following the directions of the prophet Elisha, which required him to be immersed seven times in the Jordan River, Naaman was cured and returned home to Syria a worshiper of Yahweh. (2 Kings 5:1–27)

Obadiah (oh-buh-di'uh), overseer of Ahab's palace, saved the lives of 100 prophets of Yahweh by hiding them during a purge ordered by Jezebel. Obadiah's name means "servant of Yahweh." Obadiah is also the name of a later prophet and author of one of the biblical books. (1 Kings 18:3–16)

Prophet. A prophet is a person who serves as an authoritative spokesperson for God. This definition eliminates any notion that the biblical prophets were primarily fortune tellers or crystal ball gazers. The work of a prophet was based on the firm conviction that God speaks to humanity. "Thus says the Lord!" was the customary way they began their messages. There were associations of prophets in Israel from the time of Samuel (see 1 Samuel 10:5 and 19:20), but they seem to have diminished in importance as the "writing prophets," whose messages we have in the Old Testament, became prominent.

Rehoboam (ree-huh-boh'uhm), who succeeded his father King Solomon, did not inherit his wisdom. Upon Solomon's death Rehoboam decided to ignore good advice given by his father's trusted advisors. Responding instead to the counsel of his contemporaries, he increased the tax burden that was already heavy, causing a rupture between the tribes that resulted in the two kingdoms of Israel and Judah. As King of Judah, he lapsed into idol worship, fathered 88 children, and witnessed the plundering of the Temple by the Egyptian armies. (1 Kings 11:43 to 14:31)

Samaria, the third capital city of Israel, the Northern Kingdom, was built by King Omri on a high hill – its name means "place of watch." The siege of the Assyrians, under Shalamaneser and Sargon, lasted for three years, 724–721 B.C. The conquerors led over 27,000 citizens into exile and repopulated the city with foreigners brought in from other parts of the Assyrian Empire. The Samaritans of Jesus' day were descended from the mixture of Jews who remained in the area and foreigners who were brought into the land. (1 Kings 13:32; 2 Kings 3:1)

THE SEARCH BEGINS

The passages you are to read provide only the barest outline of the nearly 350 year period covered in *The Two Kingdoms*. The map, "The Kingdoms of Israel and Judah," and "The Two Kingdoms" chart, which you will find on pages 93 and 94 will help you with this confusing period of history. The notes that you make here will help you retell the story of *The Two Kingdoms*. As you read the material, use these questions to help you see "the big picture."

- *What caused the division of the United Kingdom into the two kingdoms of Israel and Judah?*
- *What role did the worship of foreign gods play in the deterioration of these two kingdoms?*
- *What seems to be the major significance of the period of the two kingdoms?*

1 Kings 12:1–20, Northern Israel Revolts

1 Kings 14:21–31, The Reign of King Rehoboam of Judah

1 Kings 18:1–46, Elijah on Mount Carmel

1 Kings 19:1–21, Elijah at Mount Sinai

2 Kings 5:1–19, Elisha and Namaan

2 Kings 9:1–13, 30–37, Elisha and Jehu's Revolution

2 Kings 17:1–18, King Hoshea and the Fall of Samaria

2 Kings 22:1–20, Josiah and the Discovery of the Book of the Law

2 Kings 24:10–20; 25:1–12 The Fall of Jerusalem

THE SEARCH CONTINUES

In these readings I have questions about...

In these readings I discovered...

FOCUSING THE SEARCH

Some verses and stories mentioned above are repeated in other books of the Bible. A Bible with marginal notes or footnotes will list these "parallel readings." Many times the parallel readings are word for word. (See 2 Chronicles 36:22–23 and Ezra 1:1–3.) In other cases, the parallel readings differ enough to place a different emphasis on the passage. This is true of the two passages you will be working with in this "Focusing the Search."

Many of the stories about the kings you have studied in this Discovery and Discovery 8 are recorded not only in 1 and 2 Samuel and 1 and 2 Kings, but also in 1 and 2 Chronicles, a writing that dates to a later time. The writer of Chronicles wrote history from a particular perspective. He was much more interested in "why" than he was in who, what, where, when, and how.

Read the two passages below. As you read, underline or highlight the material that is the same. Then answer the questions below.

THE FALL OF JERUSALEM

2 Kings 25:1–7

Zedekiah rebelled against the king of Babylon. ¹And in the ninth year of his reign, in the tenth month, on the tenth day of the month, King Nebuchadnezzar of Babylon came with all his army against Jerusalem, and laid siege to it; they built siegeworks against it all around. ²So the city was besieged until the eleventh year of King Zedekiah. ³On the ninth day of the fourth month the famine became so severe in the city that there was no food for the people of the land. ⁴Then a breach was made in the city wall; the king with all the soldiers fled by night by the way of the gate

2 Chronicles 36:13–21

¹³He also rebelled against King Nebuchadnezzar, who had made him swear by God; he stiffened his neck and hardened his heart against turning to the LORD, the God of Israel. ¹⁴All the leading priests and the people also were exceedingly unfaithful, following all the abominations of the nations; and they polluted the house of the LORD that he had consecrated in Jerusalem. ¹⁵The LORD, the God of their ancestors, sent persistently to them by his messengers, because he had compassion on his people and on his dwelling place; ¹⁶but they kept mocking the messengers of God, despising

between the two walls, by the king's garden, though the Chaldeans were all around the city. They went in the direction of the Arabah. ⁵But the army of the Chaldeans pursued the king, and overtook him in the plains of Jericho; all his army was scattered, deserting him. ⁶Then they captured the king and brought him up to the king of Babylon at Riblah, who passed sentence on him. ⁷They slaughtered the sons of Zedekiah before his eyes, then put out the eyes of Zedekiah; they bound him in fetters and took him to Babylon.

his words, and scoffing at his prophets, until the wrath of the LORD against his people became so great that there was no remedy. ¹⁷Therefore he brought up against them the king of the Chaldeans, who killed their youths with the sword in the house of their sanctuary, and had no compassion on young man or young woman, the aged or the feeble; he gave them all into his hand. ¹⁸All the vessels of the house of God, large and small, and the treasures of the house of the LORD, and the treasures of the king and of his officials, all these he brought to Babylon. ¹⁹They burned the house of God, broke down the wall of Jerusalem, burned all its palaces with fire, and destroyed all its precious vessels. ²⁰He took into exile in Babylon those who had escaped from the sword, and they became servants to him and to his sons until the establishment of the kingdom of Persia, ²¹to fulfill the word of the LORD by the mouth of Jeremiah, until the land had made up for its sabbaths. All the days that it lay desolate it kept sabbath, to fulfill seventy years.

1. How are the passages similar?

2. What seems to be the intent of the writer of 2 Kings?

3. What seems to be the intent of the writer of 2 Chronicles?

4. How might this information influence your study of the Bible?

If you are interested in further research, you can also look at the third account of the fall of Jerusalem in Jeremiah 52:3b-11.

PUTTING IT TOGETHER

The history of the two Kingdoms of Israel and Judah is difficult to follow. Yet even though the people, events, and places are interwoven in the biblical stories, there is a common thread. This common thread is easy to discover because it is repeated many times: the success of the nation depends upon its faithfulness to God.

As you discovered in the previous session, the kings of Israel did not enjoy the "absolute" power usually given to rulers. Their power came from God and they were subject to the same laws that governed the people they ruled. This also meant that the kings of Israel and Judah were not judged by the same standards as other kings. In other cultures the evaluation of a king's rule might be based upon the kingdom's growth, economy, and victories. For the kings of Israel and Judah a different "yardstick" was used. Using the passages noted below in the "King's Report Card," read about five kings of Israel and five kings of Judah to discover what that "yardstick" was. Be sure to "grade" each of the kings listed. Under "comments" indicate the words in the passage that convinced you the "grade" should be awarded.

THE KING'S REPORT CARD

GRADING: *O = OUTSTANDING*   *S = SATISFACTORY*   *P = POOR*

Northern Kingdom – Israel

King	Reference	O	S	P	Comments
Nadab	1 Kings 15:25–26	___	___	___	_____
Baasha	1 Kings 15:33–34	___	___	___	_____
Omri	1 Kings 16:23–26	___	___	___	_____
Jehu	2 Kings 10:28–31	___	___	___	_____
Hoshea	2 Kings 17:1–2	___	___	___	_____

Southern Kingdom – Judah

King	Reference	O	S	P	Comments
Jehoshaphat	1 Kings 22:41–44	___	___	___	_____
Jehoram	2 Kings 8:16–19	___	___	___	_____
Hezekiah	2 Kings 18:1–8	___	___	___	_____
Josiah	2 Kings 22:1–2	___	___	___	_____
Jehoiakim	2 Kings 23:35–37	___	___	___	_____

What was the yardstick used to measure whether a king was "good" or "bad"?

REFLECTION

1. Reflect upon the impact of God's revelation to Elijah on Mount Sinai. It was traditionally thought that God spoke out of earthquake, fire, and wind. Instead, God spoke to Elijah in an unexpected way. In what ways do you think God speaks today? In what ways has God spoken to you?

2. Consider the temptation of the Israelites to worship idols and to indulge in pagan religious rites. In what ways are God's people still tempted by idols and torn between faith in God and faith in rival gods?

The Kingdoms of Israel and Judah

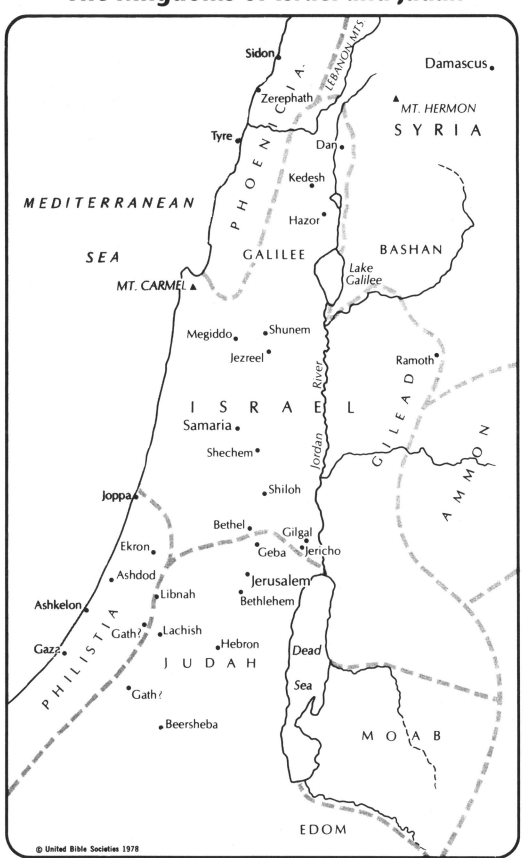

THE TWO KINGDOMS

THE KINGDOM OF ISRAEL		THE KINGDOM OF JUDAH
c.922-901 JEROBOAM	922	REHOBOAM c.922-915
	920	
	910	ABIJAH c.915-913
c.901-900 NADAB	900	
c.900-877 BAASHA	890	ASA c.913-873
c.877-876 ELAH	880	
c.876 ZIMRI		
c.876-869 OMRI	870	
c.869-850 AHAB	860	JEHOSHAPHAT c.873-849
c.850-849 AHAZIAH	850	JEHORAM c.849-842
c.849-842 JEHORAM	840	AHAZIAH c.842
		ATHALIAH c.842-837
c.842-815 JEHU	830	
	820	JOASH c.837-800
	810	
c.815-801 JEHOAHAZ	800	
c.801-786 JEHOASH	790	AMAZIAH c.800-783
	780	
c.786-746 JEROBOAM II	770	UZZIAH c.783-742

THE KINGDOM OF ISRAEL   ## THE KINGDOM OF JUDAH

760

750 ········

c.746-745 ZECHARIAH ········
      c.745 SHALLUM ········   JOTHAM c.750-735
c.745-738 MENAHEM   740
c.738-737 PEKAHIAH ::::::::
   c.737-732 PEKAH ········   ········
                         730
  c.732-724 HOSHEA   JEHOAHAZ c.735-715

721 FALL OF SAMARIA ::::::::
                         720
                         ········

710

700   HEZEKIAH c.715-687

690 ········

680

670   MANASSEH 687-642

660

650

640 :::::::: AMON 642-640

630

620   JOSIAH 640-609

610
          :::::::: JEHOAHAZ II 609
               JEHOIAKIM 609-598
600 :::::::: JEHOIACHIN 598-597

590   ZEDEKIAH 597-587

586 ········ FALL OF JERUSALEM

The symbol for *The Prophets* is grapes and a vine, representing Isaiah's vision of Israel as God's vineyard.

The Prophets

THE STORY CONTINUES

With what shall I come before the LORD, and bow myself before God on high?...He has told you, O mortal, what is good; and what does the LORD require of you but to do justice, and to love kindness, and to walk humbly with your God? Micah 6:6,8

Who speaks for God? Samuel, as a key leader of the people, combines the functions of a judge and a prophet. As a judge, he rules; as a prophet, he interprets the mind and will of God to the people. When the functions of judge are taken over by the kings, the role of prophet is carried on by a succession of persons who act as adviser to and critics of the monarchy and the people. Some "prophets" are "yes-men," while others are courageously and outspokenly critical. The clashes between them are vividly shown in the case of Michaiah (1 Kings 22:1–36), who speaks the truth even when it means opposing the kings and being reviled by the official prophets. Elijah and Elisha are also in this courageous tradition.

Beginning in the eighth century B.C., the things that these "speakers for God" say and do begin to be compiled in books to which their names are attached. These books make up the latter part of the Old Testament from Isaiah on. At the beginning of this period, the Northern Kingdom of Israel and the Southern Kingdom of Judah are weakened by their division and become prey, first to Egypt, Syria, and Assyria, and later to Babylon and Persia. During this tumultuous time, God speaks through the prophets, who call for obedience to the covenant and a greater commitment to love and justice.

The prophets – Micah, Amos, Hosea, and Isaiah – courageously proclaim the word of God to the two kingdoms, which are torn apart by political intrigues and defiled by impure religious practices. Micah not only asks the challenging question, "...what does the LORD require of you?," but proclaims the demanding answer, the LORD requires you "to do justice, and to love kindness, and to walk humbly with your God." (Micah 6:8)

The prophets' message has two parts. First, they remind the rulers and the people that they will be saved only by obedience to God, not by worshiping other gods or making political alliances. They accurately predict that failure to obey God will bring on disaster. Second, the prophets proclaim that simply going through the religious rituals is not enough; the kings and the people must act with love, justice, and mercy. They warn that callousness to individual human needs causes national disaster. For almost four hundred years many voices are heard in the land: the kings, the advisors, the people, the conquerors, the rich and poor. Who is heard? Who speaks for God? Is anyone listening to the "Thus says the Lord" messages of Micah, Isaiah, Amos, and Hosea? Time will tell.

PREPARING FOR THE SEARCH

The messages of these prophets are the focus of this Discovery. To learn more about the books in the Bible with the prophets' names, read the "Introduction" to each book in a study Bible or in the American Bible Society's *Today's English Version*.

Amos, a shepherd and dresser of sycamore trees, became one of the eighth century's mightiest prophets. Though a resident of Tekoa in the Southern Kingdom of Judah, Amos was called to deliver God's message to those in Bethel in the Northern Kingdom of Israel. Usually considered to be the first of the writing prophets, Amos spoke against the evil, unethical practices of the people and spoke for God's righteousness and universal sovereignty.

Hosea (hoh-zay'uh) prophesied in the years prior to Israel's collapse at the hands of the Assyrians. He was a contemporary of Isaiah, who prophesied in Judah. In 721 B.C. when Samaria, its capital city, was conquered, the Northern Kingdom came to an end. Like other prophets, Hosea proclaimed

BCE	c. 1900			1250	1210
	Patriarchs Abraham Isaac Jacob Joseph			**the Exodus** Moses Aaron Miriam	**the Conquest and Settlement** Joshua the Judges Samuel

10   98

that Israel was being punished because she was unfaithful to God. To make his point he compared Israel's unfaithfulness to that of his unfaithful wife, Gomer. Hosea used symbolic actions to communicate his message. He named a daughter "Not pitied" (Hosea 1:6) and a son "Not my people" (Hosea 1:9).

Isaiah (i-zay'uh), son of Amoz, came from an influential family in Judah and may have been a priest in the Temple. He lived in the middle of the 8th century B.C., a time of great turmoil, when Assyria was at the height of its power. Isaiah urged the kings of Judah to put their trust in God and spoke against their attempts to secure peace by foreign alliances. He looked forward to a future leader who would guide the nation into righteous and faithful living. Many scholars believe that only Chapters 1–39 of the book that bears his name are the work of the son of Amoz. Because the contents of Chapters 40–59 reflect a setting during the exile, they are usually attributed to a follower or disciple of Isaiah. Chapters 60–66 are set in a time after the exile and are likewise attributed to one of Isaiah's disciples.

Micah, a contemporary of Isaiah and Hosea, prophesied in Judah, the Southern Kingdom, in the eighth century B.C. Like the other prophets he took the people to task for their immorality, especially of the rich toward the poor, and for turning away from God's requirements – justice and mercy.

THE SEARCH BEGINS

God's prophets Isaiah, Hosea, Amos and Micah used powerful words to declare their messages. Sometimes these words were ones of doom and despair. At other times their proclamations offered hope. Always, they spoke of God's constant love for the people. Each message was filled with vivid images and powerful similes. As you make your notes, think about the message that is being delivered and answer these questions:

- *What will happen?*
- *Why will it happen?*
- *What must be done?*
- *Is this a message of hope, doom, or both?*

1030	930		722/721	587/586	538	333	63
Monarchy Founded	**Divided Kingdom**	Elisha	**Fall of Samaria**	**Fall of Jerusalem**	**Return and Restoration**	**Greek Rule**	**Roman Rule**
Saul	Jeroboam	Jehu	Josiah	**Exile in**	Haggai	Daniel written	
David	Rehoboam	Amos	Zephaniah	**Babylon**	Zechariah		
Solomon	Ahab	Hosea		Ezekiel	Ezra		
	Elijah	Micah			Nehemiah		
		1 Isaiah					

Amos 1:1–2; 2:4–3:2, God Judges Judah and Israel

Amos 5:4–24, Repent!

Amos 7:1–17, Visions

Hosea 1:1–2:1, God's Message to Hosea

Hosea 6:1–6, Know the Lord

Hosea 11:1–11, God's Tender Love

Micah 6:1–8, What the Lord Requires

Isaiah 1:1–20, The Lord Says

Isaiah 5:1–7, The Vineyard

Isaiah 9:2–7, The Future Ruler

THE SEARCH CONTINUES

In these readings I have questions about...

In these readings I discovered...

FOCUSING THE SEARCH

One of the most visually vivid passages in the Old Testament is Isaiah 6:1–13. In this passage Isaiah reports how he was "called" from his occupation as a priest to become a prophet. Words alone could not explain what must have been an overwhelming experience. However, through the words that describe this vision of Isaiah, we can gain a small understanding of how he felt. Read Isaiah 6:1–13.

Our present worship services use some of the same elements found in this passage, although not necessarily in the same order. Indicate the verses you feel can be considered:

Call to Worship _____

Praise and Adoration _____

Confession of Sin _____

Assurance of Pardon _____

Message _____

Call to Service _____

Response _____

PUTTING IT TOGETHER

Prophets play a very important role in the Old Testament. As "speakers for God," they were called to proclaim the message to the people. The role was seldom received with enthusiasm, since being a prophet was neither popular nor safe. Nevertheless, the prophets, including Isaiah, Hosea, Amos, and Micah, went where God sent them and spoke the words God gave them.

The passages you just read give a clear picture of the type of "work" prophets did. Based on that information, prepare a help-wanted ad for the position of PROPHET. Use your imagination. The newspaper ads on the following page may give you some ideas.

HELP WANTED – PROPHET

REFLECTION

1. Think over God's tender words to Hosea: "When Israel was a child, I loved him... I led them with cords of human kindness, with bands of love. I was to them like those who lift infants to their cheeks. I bent down to them and fed them." (Hosea 11:1,4)

What do these words say to you about God? How has your experience of love from friend, family, or spouse influenced the ways you experience and understand God's love?

2. Reflect upon God's powerful words to Amos: "I hate, I despise your festivals and I take no delight in your solemn assemblies... But let justice roll down like waters, and righteousness like an everflowing stream." (Amos 5:21, 24)

In what ways are these ancient words still addressed to the people of God today? What do you think it takes for justice and righteousness to flow from you; from others; from the church?

The symbol for *The Exile* is a chain, representing the chains which bound the captives led into Babylon. (Jeremiah 40:1)

DISCOVERY 11

The Exile

THE STORY CONTINUES

I am about to do a new thing; now it springs forth, do you not perceive it? Isaiah 43:19

The message of the prophets goes unheeded and disaster follows. For two years, 587–586 B.C., Nebuchadnezzar and his Babylonian army besiege Jerusalem, starving the people out, and destroying them by superior strength. The Southern Kingdom of Judah falls to the Babylonians just as the Northern Kingdom of Israel fell to the Assyrians 135 years earlier. Zedekiah, the last king of Judah, watches as his sons, successors to the throne of David, are killed, and is then himself blinded and taken into captivity. Jerusalem is destroyed with the Temple, built 400 years earlier, left in ruins. Nebuchadnezzar takes many of Judah's citizens, as well as much of Jerusalem's wealth, back to Babylon. The Exile begins.

As the years in exile pass, God's ancient promises are remembered, and the people mourn for their future. God promised them a home; yet they are living once again in a foreign country. God promised them many descendants; yet their families are scattered and in captivity. God promised to be their God and gave them the Law; yet God's Temple is in ruins. What is the meaning of all that has happened?

In the midst of this national tragedy three prophets – Jeremiah, Isaiah of the Exile, and Ezekiel – proclaim God's future promise, "Behold, I make all things new!" They declare that God is using Babylon to punish Judah for its sins, but only for a limited time. Since God is always faithful to the covenant, the people must anticipate the new future God is creating. It is a difficult message to hear in exile: the foundations and the framework of Israel's faith have been shaken. Yet God sets about creating all things new and uses some unlikely people and events to accomplish the divine purpose.

PREPARING FOR THE SEARCH

Cyrus, King of the Persians, conquered the Babylonians in 539–8 B.C. Although he was not a Jew, Cyrus was proclaimed as God's anointed (messiah) by Isaiah. The prophet viewed him as God's agent in freeing the Jews from the Babylonians and permitting them to return to Jerusalem.

Exile. When the Northern Kingdom of Israel was conquered by Assyria in 721 B.C., many inhabitants were taken into exile. When the Babylonians overthrew the Assyrians and captured Jerusalem in 597 B.C. and 586 B.C., many of the people were taken into exile in Babylon. Exile lasted until 538 B.C. when the Persians, under Cyrus, conquered the Babylonians and Cyrus permitted those in exile very gradually to return to their country.

Ezekiel (ee-zee' kee-uhl), a prophet who had also been a priest, was active from 597 B.C., when he was sent into exile in Babylonia, until about 571 B.C. During the exile he spoke God's word, often using symbolic actions and mysterious imagery. He spent much of his life ministering to the other captives. Ezekiel looked forward to the future restoration of the renewed people.

Isaiah of the Exile. Chapters 40–55 in the Book of Isaiah depict a time in the life of Israel many decades later than Chapters 1–39. The author of these prophetic messages addresses those who are in exile in a foreign land with a proclamation of hope·and comfort. He uses the metaphor of the "servant of the Lord" several times. This seems to be a many-sided concept and may represent the nation Israel, a righteous leader, or the messiah. For Christians the concept of the servant is fulfilled in Jesus of Nazareth, who now leads a servant people. Scholars refer to this prophet as the Isaiah of the Exile, Second Isaiah, or Deutero-Isaiah.

Jeremiah was born in the middle of the seventh century B.C. to a priestly family in Anathoth, a village near Jerusalem. His prophetic ministry began a few years before the book of the law was discovered in the Temple, and concluded during the time of the Babylonian exile, around 586 B.C. Jeremiah's scribe, Baruch, was responsible for both writing down Jeremiah's prophecies and reading them to the people publicly.

BCE	c. 1900			1250	1210
	Patriarchs			**the**	**the**
	Abraham			**Exodus**	**Conquest**
	Isaac			Moses	**and**
	Jacob			Aaron	**Settlement**
	Joseph			Miriam	Joshua
					the Judges
					Samuel

Nebuchadnezzar (ne' buh-kuhd-nez' uhr) became King of Babylon in 605 B.C., just twenty-one years after the Neo-Babylonian Empire had been founded by his father. The ultimate ill-fated revolt by King Zedekiah resulted in Nebuchadnezzar's taking Jerusalem in 586 B.C., the burning of the Temple, and the captivity of many people. This period is known as the Babylonian Captivity or Exile.

Zedekiah, son of Josiah, was appointed vassal King of Judah by Nebuchadnezzar in 597 B.C. During the siege of Jerusalem he tried to escape from the city. He was captured, made to watch as his sons were put to death, then blinded and put in prison in Babylon until his death. (2 Kings 24–25; Jeremiah 21,32,34, 37–39)

THE SEARCH BEGINS

As you read these passages related to *The Exile,* remember that in the first four of them Jeremiah is speaking to people not yet conquered by Babylon. In Jeremiah 31:15–34, however, he is speaking to those who have been taken into captivity. The prophecies of Ezekiel and Isaiah of the Exile are delivered in Babylon to a people without much hope.

As you make the notes for retelling the story of *The Exile,* keep these questions in mind.

- *How did the prophets both challenge and comfort the people before and during their exile in Babylon?*
- *How was the conquest by Babylon seen as God's punishment?*
- *In what ways were the prophets' messages similar? Different?*

Jeremiah 1:1–10, The Call of Jeremiah

1030	930		722/721	587/586	538		333		63
Monarchy Founded	**Divided Kingdom**	Elisha	**Fall of Samaria**	**Fall of Jerusalem**	**Return and Restoration**		**Greek Rule**		**Roman Rule**
Saul	Jeroboam	Jehu	Josiah	**Exile in**	Haggai		Daniel written		
David	Rehoboam	Amos	Zephaniah	**Babylon**	Zechariah				
Solomon	Ahab	Hosea		Ezekiel	Ezra				
	Elijah	Micah			Nehemiah				
		1 Isaiah							

Jeremiah 2:1–13, God's Message to Israel

Jeremiah 18:1–12, The Potter

Jeremiah 21:1–14, Jerusalem's Defeat

Jeremiah 31:15–34, A New Covenant

Ezekiel 1:1–3:17, Ezekiel's Vision

Ezekiel 37:1–14, The Valley of Dry Bones

Isaiah 40:1–11, Proclaim the Good News

Isaiah 43:1–21, God Promises Rescue

Isaiah 45:1–13, God Chooses Cyrus

Isaiah 52:13–53:12, The Suffering Servant

THE SEARCH CONTINUES

In these readings I have questions about...

In these readings I discovered...

FOCUSING THE SEARCH

In this course you have already looked at a number of Bible study "tools," such as a concordance, cross reference notes, footnotes, and parallel readings. Another tool that is used by pastors and lay people is a Bible commentary. Commentaries are written by scholars who have spent many years studying one part of the Bible. Among other things, they give important historical information that affects the interpretation of a text.

Commentaries come in different forms. There are commentaries that only deal with one book of the Bible. Examples include Walter Brueggemann's commentary on *Genesis* and the commentary on *1 Corinthians* by William Orr and James Walther. Others, such as the *Interpreter's Bible Commentary* and *The Layman's Bible Commentary*, cover all of the books of the Bible and contain many volumes. A third type is a one-volume commentary, such as *The Interpreter's One-Volume Commentary on the Bible* and *Harper's Bible Commentary*. As you can imagine, these very thick books contain information contributed by many scholars. Although the information provided is not in-depth, a one-volume commentary can be extremely helpful.

Below is a portion of the information about the book of Ezekiel in *Harper's Bible Commentary*. Read Ezekiel 37:1–14 again. Then read the information from the commentary.

37:1–14, The Valley of Dry Bones. Ezekiel's dramatic vision of the valley filled with dry bones is undated, but it must have been received after the Exile had been under way long enough for the people to have lost their hope of ever returning to the land. Unlike the prophet's earlier visions (1:1–3:15; chaps. 8–11), this one is allegorical. However, the prophet still follows his usual practice of leading his readers through the vision as he experienced it (37:1–10). Only after the vision has been described in all of its complexity does he provide an interpretation (vv. 11–14).

The vision begins when God transports the prophet by means of the Spirit (cf. 3:12–15; 8:3) and brings him to a valley or plain, presumably the same plain where Ezekiel saw his initial vision of God's presence in Babylon (1:1–3:15). The valley is full of bones, which have lain on the ground long enough for them to have been stripped of their flesh and dried by the sun. God leads the prophet on a tour through the valley, and he is impressed by the number and dry condition of the bones. God then asks the prophet if the bones can be made to live again. The prophet seems genuinely surprised at the question, since the reanimation of such old bones seems out of the question, and he replies that only God can answer that question. By way of response to the prophet,

God invites Ezekiel to participate directly in the vision rather than simply observing it. He is to prophesy to the bones and command them to reassemble themselves and clothe themselves with flesh. When the prophet does what God commands, the bones begin to arrange themselves in their proper order with a noise that shakes the valley, and then they array themselves with flesh. The prophet is then ordered to prophesy to the Spirit, which enters the bones and reanimates them (vv. 1–10; cf. Gen. 2:7). Just as in an earlier vision Ezekiel's prophetic word began the judgment and death of the people (Ezek. 11:13), so now his word helps to restore the nation. In the history of Israel, God speaking through the prophet is the one who kills and the one who gives life.

Scholars have sometimes assumed that Ezekiel's striking image of the dry bones was drawn from his actual observation of battlefields, but the real source of the image is to be found in the interpretation of the allegory (37:11–14). The exiles, who feel that they have been cut off from God, have been lamenting that their bones have dried up and their hope for restoration destroyed (cf. Ps. 31:10; Prov. 17:22). Without God's presence they consider themselves virtually dead. However, God promises to open the graves of the exiles, to reanimate them with the divine Spirit, and to return them to their land.

Although the interpretation in Ezek. 37:11–14 seems to have originally understood the opening of Israel's graves as yet another literary image describing God's restoration of the exiles, later Jewish and Christian interpreters understood the image literally and saw in the passage a reference to the actual resurrection of the dead. The language of vv. 12–13 is vague enough to support both interpretations, and the more literal interpretation may even have been in the mind of Ezekiel and his disciples.

How does this material help you understand the passage better? If you want to see how other commentaries treat this passage, check your church library or ask your church staff.

PUTTING IT TOGETHER

"Do not remember the former things, or consider the things of old. I am about to do a new thing; now it springs forth, do you not perceive it?" (Isaiah 43:18–19)

The prophets of the Exile – Ezekiel, Isaiah, and Jeremiah – all proclaimed God's promise of a new future for the people of Israel and Judah. Imagine you are one of the exiled Jews living in Babylon and listen to the prophets' words as if for the first time.

You hear a message from the prophet Isaiah that begins, *"Comfort, O comfort my people, says your God."* (Isaiah 40:1)

You hear a message from the prophet Jeremiah that begins, *"Keep your voice from weeping, and your eyes from tears."* (Jeremiah 31:16)

You hear a message from the prophet Ezekiel that begins, *"I am going to open your graves, and bring you up from your graves, O my people; and I will bring you back to the land of Israel."* (Ezekiel 37:12)

Write a short letter to one of your friends back in Jerusalem. (Not all of the people were forced into exile in Babylon.) Share how you have been feeling in exile, what you have heard from the prophets, and how you feel about these messages of comfort and hope.

Dear _____ ,

Sincerely, _____

REFLECTION

1. Reflect upon Ezekiel's vision of the valley of dry bones, a vision that vividly depicts the breath that God breathes into all that lives. What dry bones do you see in our world that need God's creative Spirit? What are the dry bones in your life that need new life?

2. Think over God's words to Isaiah: "Surely he has borne our infirmities and carried our diseases; yet we accounted him stricken, struck down by God, and afflicted. But he was wounded for our transgressions, crushed for our iniquities; upon him was the punishment that made us whole, and by his bruises we are healed." (Isaiah 53:4–5)

What do you think this passage meant to those who first heard Isaiah's words? What do you think these words meant over 500 years later to those who knew Jesus? What does God say to you today in these words?

The symbol for *The Return* is a Jerusalem gate, representing the entry back into Jerusalem and the opportunity to rebuild. (Nehemiah 3:13–15)

The Return

THE STORY CONTINUES

Who gave you a decree to build this house and to finish this structure? Ezra 5:3b

What does the future hold for Jerusalem? Nothing less than rebuilding and restoration! In 538 B.C., Cyrus, King of Persia, issues an edict permitting the Jews in Babylon to return to Jerusalem. An enlightened ruler, he believes it is better for all the exiles in Persian-conquered territory to return to their native countries. Some Israelites, because of their faith in God, believe that Cyrus has been brought to power for just this purpose. During the next twenty years a large number choose to leave Babylon. However, many remain because they have built homes and new lives for themselves there. Starting over again in a country they have never seen is too difficult. Although thousands do return to Jerusalem, the work is slow, and the old glory known as the Kingdom of Judah is not recaptured. Judah remains a small, insignificant part of the greater Persian Empire.

One hundred years later the fortifications of the city are still in ruins. In 439 B.C, Nehemiah begins the task of rebuilding the walls of Jerusalem, and Ezra sets about rebuilding the religious life of the nation. Nehemiah's efforts not only restore the city, but also develop a strong sense of community. Ezra's focus on reforming religious practice and promoting racial purity helps maintain the community's identity as Jews. But to those who remember God's call to be "a light to the nations," there is great concern about the call for separatism (freeing themselves from foreign elements, and maintaining strict obedience to the law of Moses). Ruth and Jonah, stories set in the past, are written to offset the move toward racial purity and separatism by reminding Israel of God's love for all the nations. Even so, Israel's identity is increasingly defined by a strict adherence to following the commandments, ordinances, and statutes of the Law.

PREPARING FOR THE SEARCH

These definitions will help you understand the story of *The Return.*

Artaxerxes (ahr-tuh-zerk' sees), the King of Persia, allowed Ezra and other exiles to return to Jerusalem in 458 B.C. Fourteen years later he permitted Nehemiah, a servant of his court, to journey to Jerusalem to rebuild the city's walls. In 433 B.C. Nehemiah, who had briefly returned to Persia, was given permission once again by Artaxerxes to revisit Jerusalem and become its governor.

Boaz was a wealthy land-owner in Bethlehem. He married Ruth, a woman from Moab, after her husband, his distant cousin, died.

Ezra, a priest and scribe, went to Jerusalem in 458 B.C. to rebuild the Jewish community. Nehemiah was commissioned to rebuild the walls of the city. Ezra's efforts in conforming the Jewish community to Mosaic law set Judaism on the course which it has maintained to this day – especially in focusing on maintenance of the ethnic community and the distinctiveness of the Jewish tradition.

Isaiah after the Exile. Chapters 56–66 in the Book of Isaiah reflect a time after the exile; the setting of the book has moved from 6th century Babylonia to 5th century Jerusalem. The prophet (called the Isaiah after the Exile, or Third Isaiah) proclaims a future hope for a world which experiences the glory of God.

Jews. This name for the people of Israel became common after the Babylonian exile.

Jonah is the story of a prophet in Israel who was called to go to Nineveh in Assyria to proclaim the message of repentance. He was a very reluctant prophet who had trouble understanding God's compassionate concern for non-Jews. The story is an ancient one which may have been written in its current form when the Jews returned from exile in Babylon. If this is the case, it served as a powerful statement against the exclusivism being promoted at that time.

BCE	c. 1900		1250	1210
	Patriarchs Abraham Isaac Jacob Joseph		**the Exodus** Moses Aaron Miriam	**the Conquest and Settlement** Joshua the Judges Samuel

Levites (lee' vits) were those men from the tribe of Levi who were given the responsibility for the worship and rites associated with the Temple. God honored the tribe of Levi with the priesthood because they had returned their allegiance to God after the Israelites made the golden calf.

Moab, the country southwest of Israel and the Dead Sea, was named for the descendants of Moab, son of Lot. During the exodus from Egypt they refused to permit the Israelites to pass through their region and later became antagonists of Israel. Ruth was from Moab.

Naomi, mother-in-law of Ruth, returned to Bethlehem after her son died, taking Ruth with her. There she arranged Ruth's marriage to Boaz.

Nehemiah, a civil servant in Persia, was commissioned Governor of Judah by Artaxerxes. He led the people in fortifying and rebuilding Jerusalem. Nehemiah was a contemporary of Ezra and worked with him in renewing the religious life of the community.

Ruth, widow of Mahlon of Bethlehem, was from Moab. Through her mother-in-law Naomi's efforts she married Boaz, a relative of her first husband. As King David's great-grandmother, Ruth is one of four women Matthew mentions in Jesus' family tree. As a non-Jew, her story served to counter the move toward Jewish racial exclusivism after the Babylonian Exile.

Tarshish, Jonah's attempted destination in running from God's command, is thought to suggest a location in southern Spain near Gibraltar.

THE SEARCH BEGINS

The story of *The Return* covers a complicated period in the history of the people of Israel. There is very little information to help us. The country of Judah was in ruins and the population, which had once exceeded 250,000 prior to the exile, had dwindled to fewer than 20,000. After their release, the people returned slowly to the land of their ancestors. It took many years for the rebuilding of the Temple and city to be accomplished. As you read the passages, think about these questions:

- *What things occurred that made it possible for the Jews to return to Jerusalem?*
- *What happened to their faith because of the exile and the return?*
- *What caused the movement toward exclusivism?*

1030	930		722/721	587/586	538		333	63
Monarchy Founded	**Divided Kingdom**	Elisha	**Fall of Samaria**	**Fall of Jerusalem**	**Return and Restoration**		**Greek Rule**	**Roman Rule**
Saul	Jeroboam	Jehu	Josiah	**Exile in**	Haggai		Daniel written	
David	Rehoboam	Amos	Zephaniah	**Babylon**	Zechariah			
Solomon	Ahab	Hosea		Ezekiel	Ezra			
	Elijah	Micah			Nehemiah			
		1ˑIsaiah						

Ezra 1:1–2:2, The Exiles Return

Ezra 3:8–13; 4:24—5:5; 6:14–15, The Temple is Rebuilt

Ezra 6:16–22, The Passover is Celebrated

Ezra 7:1–28, Ezra Arrives in Jerusalem

Nehemiah 1:1–2:20, Nehemiah Goes to Jerusalem

Nehemiah 8:1–12, Ezra Reads the Law

Nehemiah 13:15–31, Nehemiah's Reforms

Isaiah 60:1–7, The Glorious Future

Isaiah 61:1–4, Good News is Announced

Isaiah 65:17–25, The New Creation

THE SEARCH CONTINUES

In these readings I have questions about...

In these readings I discovered...

FOCUSING THE SEARCH

Most of the stories, songs, and poems in the Bible were told and retold long before they were written down. It is therefore difficult, but not impossible, to date with certainty many of the biblical books. Biblical scholars closely examine such things as significant names, words, and events to try to determine the date of a text. Yet, even after extensive research, scholars do not always agree.

Imagine that you are a biblical scholar trying to determine the dates of the books of Jonah or Ruth. Read what one scholar has written concerning Jonah:

> This message fits best the post-exilic time in Judah, when strong nationalistic, exclusivist emphases were dominant, particularly under Ezra and Nehemiah. Jewish men were forced to divorce foreign wives, Jewish worship was closed to participation by foreigners, and blood purity was highly regarded. Some large-hearted writer, through a story about the past, sought to broaden the outlook of his narrow-minded contemporaries by portraying God as God actually is and Jews as they ought to be.
>
> Edward P. Blair, *Illustrated Bible Handbook*, p. 194

The same author says the book of Ruth may have been written:

> ...to protest against the policy of exclusion of foreigners carried out by Ezra and Nehemiah (Neh. 13:1–3, 23–27; *cf.* Ezra 10) by showing that God blessed the union of a Jew and a Moabitess with the gift of Obed, the grandfather of David.
>
> Blair, p. 130.

First read Nehemiah, chapter 13. Then, read either Jonah or Ruth and respond to the following questions.

> *a.* What evidence, if any, do you see that supports Blair's conclusions?

b. What seems to be the purpose of the book?

c. If Blair's conclusion is correct, what message does the book deliver about "foreigners?"

d. What does this book seem to say about strict adherence to Jewish law?

PUTTING IT TOGETHER

Sorting out the events of *The Return* can be frustrating. Number the following "headline news" captions to indicate the order in which they occurred. For help refer to the passages you read in "The Search Begins."

Order	Event	Order	Event
_____	**SEVEN DAY HOLIDAY DECLARED** *Jerusalem:* A year after the dedication of the Temple, the Passover is once again being celebrated in the land. This week-long festival will be observed by all Jews.	_____	**JUDAH FOR JEWS CAMPAIGN BEGINS** *Jerusalem:* "Renewal of the Covenant requires divorce of foreign wives!" declares Ezra. This decree is not met with universal enthusiasm.
_____	**HOME AT LAST!** *Jerusalem:* Ezra, fellow priests, Temple musicians, and Levites have returned to Jerusalem with the blessing of Artaxerxes to see that God's Law is obeyed.	_____	**TEMPLE PROJECT COMPLETED** *Jerusalem:* After five years of labor, the Temple project has finally been completed.
_____	**EXIT VISAS GRANTED** *Babylon:* Cyrus, King of Persia, has ordered the release of the Jews. They will be allowed to return to Judah, their homeland, taking with them their Temple treasures.	_____	**VAST BUILDING PROJECT PROPOSED** *Jerusalem:* Nehemiah has led a group of Jews back to Jerusalem. He plans to rebuild the walls of the city!

REFLECTION

1. Consider the meaning of God's good news to those who returned to Israel after exile:

"For I am about to create new heavens and a new earth; the former things shall not be remembered or come to mind. But be glad and rejoice forever in what I am creating; for I am about to create Jerusalem as a joy, and its people as a delight." (Isaiah 65: 17–18)

What do you think those who journeyed from Babylon to Jerusalem were expecting? What do you think they heard in Isaiah's message? In what ways does Isaiah's message about God's new creation cause you to rejoice?

2. Think about the story of Ruth or Jonah. Religious fanaticism has caused some people to commit atrocities in the name of their faith. What does this book say to those who defend vicious deeds by claiming they are acting for God? What does this book say to you?

The symbol for *The Law* is a Menorah, a seven-branched lampstand used in the Temple. (Zechariah 4:2)

DISCOVERY 13

The Law

THE STORY CONTINUES

So you shall remember and do all my commandments, and you shall be holy to your God. Numbers 15:40

"Remember" is one of the most important words in the faith of Israel. To remember is to be rooted in the past. To remember is to remain faithful to God's commands. To remember is to keep hoping in God's promises. Every day, month, and year, in both simple and extravagant observances, the people of Israel remember God's Law, and remember who they are and whose they are.

Before the exile, the Law, given by God to Moses, is interpreted and expanded by priests and rabbis to encompass almost every situation in life. The Law is followed in matters as private as personal hygiene and as public as the relationships between nations. To observe the Law means to keep the commandments, ordinances and statutes, and to celebrate the festivals. Every experience of worship and every festival observance is an opportunity to remember God's deliverance and God's providence.

During the exile in Babylon, perhaps the greatest threat to the faith of Israel is the threat to forget. Yet, within that pagan land, facing the lure of rival gods, they remember God's Law. In fact, the priests preserve and protect God's Law, the Torah, to maintain their identity as the people of God. After the exile the Law is more strictly interpreted, narrowly defined, and vigorously defended, as if to set apart the people of Israel from their neighbors. Even then, at the heart of the Law is the great commandment that summarizes the Law, "and you shall love the LORD your God with all your heart, and with all your soul, and with all your might." (Deuteronomy 6:5)

PREPARING FOR THE SEARCH

These definitions will help you as you begin your study of *The Law*.

Day of Atonement was the only day on which the priest entered the Holy of Holies in the Temple. It was a day of fasting and repentance for the nation. A young bull, representing the priesthood, was sacrificed. Two goats were selected to represent the nation. One was sacrificed and its blood sprinkled on the mercy seat. The other was let loose in the wilderness after a ritual in which the sins of the people were symbolically placed on its head. It was to carry away the nation's sins, thus the term "scapegoat." (Leviticus 16:8–10, 20–22)

Feast of Booths (or Tabernacles), an eight-day harvest festival of thanksgiving, was also called "the feast of the LORD" (Leviticus 23:39) and "the feast of ingathering." (Exodus 34:22) During the festival, as a remembrance of the wilderness journey, the people lived in dwellings of leaves and foliage and made a pilgrimage to the Temple to offer sacrifices. In *Today's English Version* this festival is called the "Festival of Shelters." (Leviticus 23:33–44, Deuteronomy 16:13–17)

Festival of Unleavened Bread, an eight-day observation of the Exodus from Egypt, is also linked to the beginning of the barley harvest. During the festival, in which leaven was absent from their diet, the people consecrated their first-born to the Lord. Passover is the first day of the Festival of Unleavened Bread. (Exodus 13:1–16)

Feast of Weeks, also called Pentecost, was a one-day wheat harvest festival of thanksgiving that occurred fifty days after the barley harvest festival, the Festival of Unleavened Bread. After the exile this festival was also linked to God's gift of the Law (Covenant). (Leviticus 23:15–21)

Holiness, a word which indicates "separateness," differentiates between the glory and purity of God and the rest of the created world. People, objects, and actions can share in holiness as they are consecrated to God.

Leviticus, the third book in the Old Testament, received its name from the Greek title, which means "relating to the Levites." Its Hebrew name is "And he called." Leviticus, since it deals with the Levite priests, the sons of Aaron, contains ordinances and regulations for attaining holiness – ceremonial purity and moral purity.

BCE	c. 1900		1250	1210
	Patriarchs Abraham Isaac Jacob Joseph		**the Exodus** Moses Aaron Miriam	**the Conquest and Settlement** Joshua the Judges Samuel

New Year Festival is also called the "Feast of Trumpets." In Hebrew it is called "Rosh Hashanah," and was celebrated in the fall with rest and sacrifices. Trumpets announced the beginning of the new year. (Leviticus 23:24–25, Numbers 29:1–6)

Passover, a ceremonial family dinner commemorating the Exodus from Egypt, was a one-day celebration that began the Feast of Unleavened Bread. Each element of the Passover was a reminder of God's deliverance of the Jews from Egypt. Passover, the Feast of Weeks, and the Feast of Tabernacles were the three annual feasts that required attendance at the sanctuary in Jerusalem.

Sabbath, from the word meaning "to rest, to cease," is the seventh day of the Hebrew week, and one of the distinguishing marks of Israel's faith. Keeping the Sabbath as a day of rest is understood in the Ten Commandments to be a response to God's resting after creation and God's deliverance in the Exodus. The Sabbath begins at sundown on Friday and concludes at sundown on Saturday. (See Genesis 1:31—2:2.)

Torah, a Hebrew word meaning "instruction," is used as the name of the first five books of the Bible and in a more general sense to refer to any of God's laws, ordinances, and instructions.

THE SEARCH BEGINS

These passages were selected to give you an understanding of the concept of *The Law.* Make notes that answer these two questions:

- *What does the law command the people to do?*
- *Why are they to do these things?*

Exodus 34:10–28, God Renews the Covenant

1030	930		722/721	587/586	538	333	63
Monarchy Founded	**Divided Kingdom**	Elisha	**Fall of Samaria**	**Fall of Jerusalem**	**Return and Restoration**	**Greek Rule**	**Roman Rule**
Saul	Jeroboam	Jehu	Josiah	**Exile in**	Haggai	Daniel	
David	Rehoboam	Amos	Zephaniah	**Babylon**	Zechariah	written	
Solomon	Ahab	Hosea		Ezekiel	Ezra		
	Elijah	Micah			Nehemiah		
		1 Isaiah					

Leviticus 19:1–18, The Holiness Code

Deuteronomy 5:1–22, The Ten Commandments

Deuteronomy 6:1–9, The Great Commandment

Deuteronomy 6:10–25, Remember God's Faithfulness

Deuteronomy 30:1–20, Choose Life!

Psalm 1, Joy in God's Law

Psalm 19:7–14, God's Glory

THE SEARCH CONTINUES

In these readings I have questions about...

In these readings I discovered...

FOCUSING THE SEARCH

Annual celebrations are tools that help in remembering important events. Birthdays, anniversaries, and holidays, both secular and religious, as they are celebrated, recall the history that made the events important. They also help us to reflect upon the meanings those events have for us in the present.

The great national festivals of Israel were opportunities for the people to remember God's mighty acts in their past and to renew their present and future commitment to God's covenant. For each of the following festivals read at least one of the passages listed. You may also turn to the information listed in "Preparing for the Search." Under each festival, indicate the historical event that the community remembered and the manner in which the festival was celebrated.

SOME FESTIVALS OF THE JEWISH YEAR

Festival	Jewish Name	Bible References
SABBATH	*Shabbat*	Exodus 20:8–10; Leviticus 23:1–3

Event Remembered _____

_____

Manner Celebrated _____

_____

NEW YEAR	*Rosh Hashanah*	Leviticus 23:23–25; Numbers 29:1–6

Event Remembered _____

_____

Manner Celebrated _____

_____

Festival	Jewish Name	Bible References
DAY OF ATONEMENT	*Yom Kippur*	Leviticus 23:26–32; Numbers 29:7–11

Event Remembered _____

_____

Manner Celebrated _____

_____

Festival	Jewish Name	Bible References
FEAST OF BOOTHS (or Shelters)	*Sukkoth*	Leviticus 23:33–44; Nehemiah 8:13–18

Event Remembered _____

_____

Manner Celebrated _____

_____

Festival	Jewish Name	Bible References
PASSOVER and UN-LEAVENED BREAD	*Pesach*	Leviticus 23:5–14; Numbers 28:16–25

Event Remembered _____

_____

Manner Celebrated _____

_____

Festival	Jewish Name	Bible References
FESTIVAL OF WEEKS (Pentecost)	*Shavuoth*	Leviticus 23:15–22; Numbers 28:26–31

Event Remembered _____

_____

Manner Celebrated _____

_____

13

PUTTING IT TOGETHER

When the Israelites made a "statement of faith," they used words that recalled how God had been active in their past. Deuteronomy 26:5–10 is sometimes called the "Little Creed." Bernhard Anderson, in his book *Understanding the Old Testament,* calls these verses "the heart of the Pentateuch" (one name for the first five books of the Hebrew Scriptures). This creedal prayer recalls how God saved the Israelites from their enemies and fulfilled the covenant by bringing them back to the land promised to their ancestors. Read the passage carefully.

There are many formal "statements of faith" or "confessions" that are used in the church. They help us articulate what we believe about God. However, because each of us has experienced God's activity in our lives in different ways, our own personal statements of faith reflect those differences. Think about how God has been active in your life. Pretend that you need to explain your belief in God to someone who has no belief in God. Write at least four or five sentences that explain how your experiences have shaped your faith.

REFLECTION

1. Reflect upon God's gift of the Ten Commandments. Which of the commandments speaks most directly to you at this time? Which one is the most difficult for you to follow? In what ways do knowing and following the commandments draw you closer to God?

2. Relive the joy in God's Law expressed by the psalmist in Psalm 1. How does God's law refresh and nourish you? What do the images in the psalm say to you?

The symbol for *The Wisdom* is a lamp, representing an image from the Psalms depicting true wisdom. (Psalm 119:105)

DISCOVERY 14

The Wisdom

THE STORY CONTINUES

But where shall wisdom be found? And where is the place of understanding? Job 28:12

One way to look at life is to take in the big picture: empires rise and fall, kingdoms flourish and decline, leaders succeed and fail. Another way to look at life is to focus on the basics: people live and die, the sun rises and sets, the hours pass. The wisdom teachers of Israel see life this way.

Throughout the centuries there are teachers of wisdom in Israel who examine their life experiences to discover answers to provocative questions. They offer teachings and stories to respond to some of the most difficult questions people ask. How can I be happy? Why is there pain and suffering? What is the purpose of work? Is there a meaning to life? Simply asking such a question of a wisdom teacher invites a saying, a proverb, a maxim, a teaching, a story, or a poem. The answers and reflections are usually short, occasionally humorous and often profound.

Over the centuries their sayings and stories are treasured and collected. Today we read their wisdom in a number of the Psalms and the books of Proverbs, Ecclesiastes, and Job. Whereas the prophets preach extremely high ideals for faithful living, the wisdom teachers express a practical day-by-day approach. Whereas the priests prescribe rituals and festivals for the proper expression of faith, the wisdom teachers express faith in God with homespun maxims, common sense, and memorable anecdotes.

The questions the wisdom teachers address are questions all humanity shares. It is not surprising, therefore, that parallels to Israel's wisdom literature are found in Egypt and other places in the Ancient Near East. Throughout the centuries, as kingdoms rise and fall, and individuals struggle to survive, the sages offer their insights to future generations. If, in the Law, Israel separates itself from the other nations, then, in the Wisdom Literature, it is at one with the ancient world.

PREPARING FOR THE SEARCH

In preparation for reading the passages selected to illustrate *The Wisdom*, these words will be important.

Ecclesiastes is a Greek word that translated literally means "one who sits in the midst of the company (the ecclesia in Greek) and teaches or preaches." The biblical book of this name is variously ascribed to "The Preacher," "The Philosopher," or "Qoheleth," depending upon the translation.

Job. The book that bears Job's name is a major part of the wisdom literature of Israel and a revision of a very ancient tale. Job is caught in a web of forces he cannot control and that, more to his despair, he cannot even understand. Only in total trust in God does Job find any solace; he never gets the answers to the questions he asks in the beginning of the tale.

Proverb. A proverb is most often a short, wise saying, but can also be in the form of an extended poem. The Hebrew word for proverb, *mashal*, means a comparison, a likeness. The book of Proverbs is a collection of many wise sayings, maxims, comparisons, even satires.

Psalm. A psalm is a religious poem used in services of worship. The Hebrews called their collection of worship poems *Tehillim*, which means "Book of Songs of Praise." The Greek translation was *Psalmoi*, thus the current name. The 150 psalms in the Bible were collected from several periods in history and were written by several different authors. Many of the psalms are attributed to King David. The psalms not only open windows to the religious practices of Israel but also to the deep and profound feelings of the people of God. Some, like Psalms 37, 112, and 128, display a definite wisdom influence.

Satan, which literally translated means "the adversary," appears to have been part of the heavenly court. In Job, the adversary (in Hebrew it is written as "the satan"), has duties that include patrolling earth for God. Our current

BCE	c. 1900		1250	1210
	Patriarchs Abraham Isaac Jacob Joseph		**the Exodus** Moses Aaron Miriam	**the Conquest and Settlement** Joshua the Judges Samuel

popular images of Satan and the devil come from a time much later than the Old Testament.

Wisdom literature refers to those writings that focus on the practical aspects of successfully living one's life in the world. They are the writings specifically aimed at creating a moral, ethical and religious person. Proverbs, Job, Ecclesiastes, and parts of the book of Psalms are all considered to be wisdom literature.

THE SEARCH BEGINS

As you write your notes about *The Wisdom*, look for what you think is the *most important* thought, idea, or phrase in each reading and write it in the space provided. What speaks to *you* most deeply from the teachers of wisdom?

Consider these questions as you read:

- *What is wisdom?*
- *How do people become wise?*
- *What are some of the "hard questions" people in all cultures ask?*

Psalm 49, Words to the Wise

Psalm 127, Praise of God's Goodness

1030	930		722/721	587/586	538	333	63
Monarchy Founded	**Divided Kingdom**	Elisha	**Fall of Samaria**	**Fall of Jerusalem**	**Return and Restoration**	**Greek Rule**	**Roman Rule**
Saul	Jeroboam	Jehu	Josiah	**Exile in**	Haggai	Daniel	
David	Rehoboam	Amos	Zephaniah	**Babylon**	Zechariah	written	
Solomon	Ahab	Hosea		Ezekiel	Ezra		
	Elijah	Micah			Nehemiah		
		1 Isaiah					

139

14

Proverbs 1:1–7, The Beginning of Wisdom

Proverbs 19:1–29, A Collection of Sayings

Proverbs 20:1–30, More Sayings

Ecclesiastes 1:1–18, Nothing New under the Sun

Ecclesiastes 3:1–15, A Time for Everything

Ecclesiastes 9:1–12, One Fate Comes to All

Job 1:1–2:13, Job is Tested

Job 3:1–10, Job Curses His Birth

Job 38:1–18, God Responds

Job 42:1–6, Job Answers

THE SEARCH CONTINUES

In these readings I have questions about...

In these readings I discovered...

FOCUSING THE SEARCH

The entire story of Job is a search for answers. Everyone in the story asks questions: Job, Eliphaz, Bildad, Zophar, Elihu, Satan, and God. The questions they ask are disturbing, challenging, and often unanswerable. Job's questions in the midst of his suffering are some of the most perplexing. The answer that Job receives is, for him, the beginning of wisdom.

JOB: QUESTIONS AND ANSWERS

Use the following selections to focus on some of the profound questions raised in the story of Job. If you are using a Bible other than the *Revised Standard Version* or the *New Revised Standard Version*, the words at the beginning of the sentences may be different. Write the words of the questions on the lines provided.

Job 1:9....Satan to God

"Does _____

Job 2:10....Job to his wife

"Shall _____

Job 3:23....Job to himself

"Why _____

Job 4:7....Eliphaz to Job

"Who _____

Job 7:1....Job to Eliphaz

"Do not _____

_____

Job 7:17–19....Job to God

"What_____

_____

_____

Job 10:18....Job to God

"Why _____

Job 11:7....Zophar to Job

"Can _____

Job 17:15–16....Job to Zophar

"Where then _____

Job 21:7....Job to Zophar

"Why _____

Job 31:2–4....Job to himself

"What _____

"Does not _____

"Does _____

Job 38:4....God to Job

"Where _____

Job 40:2....God to Job

"Shall _____

Job 42:3....Job to God

"Who _____

"Therefore _____

Job raised many questions in his dialogue with God. What question would you ask God? How do you think God would answer? Write your reflections below.

PUTTING IT TOGETHER

Proverbs were an important part of everyday life in the ancient world. In Israel they were collected into a book of their own. They were also included in many of the other biblical writings. Select one or two of the proverbs (or any other words of wisdom from the readings for this session) that you would feel good about wearing on a T-shirt, a button, or using on a bumper sticker. What ancient "words to live by" still offer you sound advice on living a good life? Write down the wise sayings you have selected. They are to be used during the session.

REFLECTION

1. Weigh the wisdom of the preacher: "For in much wisdom is much vexation, and those who increase knowledge increase sorrow." (Ecclesiastes 1:18)

   What do these words say to you? How do the words relate to your life experience? What wisdom do you find in them?

2. Reflect upon the wisdom in Job: "Truly, the fear of the LORD, that is wisdom; and to depart from evil is understanding." (Job 28:28)

What do you think "the fear of the Lord" means? What do Job's words say to you?

The symbol for *The Visions* is the sun and moon, images dramatically depicted in visions of the future. (Joel 2:31)

The Visions

THE STORY CONTINUES

But who can endure the day of his coming, and who can stand when he appears? Malachi 3:2

Visions of the future guide the life of Israel from the very beginning. God's promise of land and descendants causes Abraham to leave his home and journey to an unknown land. God's covenant with the people of Israel at Mount Sinai creates an anticipation of security and prosperity through following commandments and observing rituals. God's covenant with David generates within the nation an expectation of an everlasting kingdom.

Visions of the future guide the people of Israel as they look forward to "The Day of the Lord" when God will fulfill the covenant promises and glorify Israel. Yet, when the Kingdom of Israel falls to the Assyrians in 721 B.C., and the Kingdom of Judah falls to the Babylonians in 586 B.C. and the Temple is destroyed, the visions change and hope is modified. The promise of land and descendants is transformed into a vision of God's ultimate restoration of both land and people. The promise of security and prosperity is transformed into a promise that will be fulfilled in the distant future. The coming "Day of the Lord" is transformed into a day of judgment when God rewards the faithful and condemns the unfaithful.

During hopeless times in Israel, when ancient promises are questioned, God inspires messages of hope. Some, such as Daniel, look to the past and write stories about one who remains faithful to God during trials and sufferings. Others, including the prophets Joel, Zechariah, Zephaniah, and

Malachi, proclaim God's messages of hope to those who feel abandoned. Their visions, which picture God's future intervention to save and rescue, promise God's future rewards to those who remain faithful.

These visions of the future, as well as other writings which are not included in our Bibles today, reflect a period of great anticipation and expectation in Israel. As the Old Testament comes to a close, those who believe that God will be faithful to the promise cannot wait to see what will happen next.

PREPARING FOR THE SEARCH

Before reading the passages associated with *The Visions*, read these definitions. Other important definitions are included in "The Search Begins" and "Focusing the Search."

Day of the Lord. Many prophets from the time of Amos spoke of "the day of the Lord." However, this idea did not originate with him. It was a popular idea held by many of God's people. Amos' contribution was to assure Israel that "the day of the Lord" was not going to be what they expected. Rather than a wonderful time when God would save them, Amos said it would be a time of darkness and punishment. Other prophets such as Obadiah and Joel understood it to be a time when God would punish nations because of their wickedness. Zephaniah 1:14–18 indicates that all of the inhabitants of the earth will be judged. There is some indication in Joel (2:30–32) and Malachi (4:5–6) that those who repent will be spared. Other expressions, such as "on that day," "the days are coming when...," or simply "then" are sometimes substituted for the phrase "the day of the Lord."

Haggai (hag' ay-i), a prophet active in Jerusalem after the exiles returned from Babylon, encouraged the people to resume rebuilding the Temple.

Visions. According to the *New Westminster Dictionary of the Bible,* there is "no sharp line of demarcation...discernible between visions and dreams." Like poetry, visions present an interpretation of reality and invite the reader or listener to share it. Cognitive insight is combined with emotional response. The fact that they were experienced and recorded to address a particular historical situation, makes it imperative that those who want to understand the biblical visions learn something about the historical context in which they were received.

BCE	c. 1900		1250	1210
	Patriarchs Abraham Isaac Jacob Joseph		**the Exodus** Moses Aaron Miriam	**the Conquest and Settlement** Joshua the Judges Samuel

Zechariah, a contemporary of Haggai, reinforced the message that the people must rebuild the Temple. Because of their encouragement, the rebuilding was completed in 516 B.C.

THE SEARCH BEGINS

These passages help you understand the purpose of *The Visions* and how they influenced the expectations of the people of Israel. These expectations were still prevalent when Jesus was born and in some ways influenced his ministry and its reception. While it is easy to get engrossed in the details of the visions, try to keep the following questions in mind as you read and let them guide the notes you take.

- *How is "the day of the Lord" described in the vision?*
- *When and where will this take place?*
- *Why is God acting to bring about such a day?*
- *Who will be punished? Who will be saved?*
- *How does the vision address the situation being faced by the people?*

Since it is important to understand the historical context in which the prophets announced their visions, the readings are preceded by some background material about the prophets and the problems they were addressing.

Joel, one of the minor prophets, lived in Judah sometime during the 5th or 4th century B.C. He was concerned about the people's lack of devotion to God. To him the drought and the locust plague that devastated the country showed God's judgment on the sinful people. He believed this punishment had been sent to call the people to repentance.

Joel 2:1–3, 10–17, The Day of the Lord

1030	930		722/721	587/586	538	333	63
Monarchy Founded	**Divided Kingdom**	Elisha	**Fall of Samaria**	**Fall of Jerusalem**	**Return and Restoration**	**Greek Rule**	**Roman Rule**
Saul	Jeroboam	Jehu	Josiah	**Exile in**	Haggai	Daniel written	
David	Rehoboam	Amos	Zephaniah	**Babylon**	Zechariah		
Solomon	Ahab	Hosea		Ezekiel	Ezra		
	Elijah	Micah			Nehemiah		
		1 Isaiah					

Joel 2:23–32, The Day of the Lord

Zephaniah prophesied shortly before the time of Josiah's religious reforms, which began in Judah in 622 B.C. To a people who had turned to idols, Zephaniah stressed the coming of "the day of the Lord," God's judgment on surrounding nations, and God's intention of saving the righteous remnant of Judah from the wrath to come.

Zephaniah 1:14—2:3, The Day of the Lord

Zephaniah 3:1–13, Jerusalem's Redemption

Zechariah and his contemporary Haggai encouraged the people to rebuild the Temple in 520–515 B.C. The book of Zechariah can be divided into two parts. Chapters 1–8 include his visions and prophecies about the future of Israel. Chapters 9–14, written by unknown authors in the 4th or 3rd centuries during the time when independence had once again been lost and the Greeks ruled the nation, deal with prophecy about God's judgment, further messages about the expected Messiah, and the establishment of a universal kingdom.

Zechariah 12:6–10, Deliverance of Jerusalem

Zechariah 14:1–9, God's Promise

Malachi, which means "my messenger" or "messenger of Yahweh," was written just before the reforms of Ezra and Nehemiah in the fifth century B.C. Because the nation had not returned to its former glory, the people believed that God had let them down. The book assures them that God loves Israel and that when the "day of the Lord" comes, the people will see how much God loves them. In the meantime their job is to remain faithful and obey the Law.

Malachi 2:17—3:5, The Day of His Coming

Malachi 4:1–6, Prepare the Way!

THE SEARCH CONTINUES

In these readings I have questions about...

In these readings I discovered...

FOCUSING THE SEARCH

Apocalyptic literature became a popular form used by writers beginning in approximately 200 B.C. It takes its name from the Greek word *apokalypsis,* meaning "to reveal." While there are apocalyptic-like sections in a number of the prophets, such as Second Isaiah, Ezekiel, and Zechariah, the most complete example of apocalyptic literature in the Old Testament is found in chapters 7–12 of the book of Daniel.

In apocalyptic writing the author employs elaborate visions that include symbolism that can only be understood by the intended readers. Because the purpose of this writing is to encourage people who are facing a time of religious crisis, this use of symbolic code ensures their safety. The book of Daniel and other apocalyptic literature remind the readers that God has been faithful in the past and assure them that God will intervene soon, although things may get worse before they get better. The message is keep the faith, trust in God, and you will be saved.

Daniel was written around 165 B.C. by an unknown prophet during the reign of Antiochus (an-ti' uh-kuhs) IV, king of Syria-Persia, who tried to stamp out Judaism. The book, which claims to be written *by* Daniel, is instead *about* Daniel, a 6th century exiled prophet who remained faithful to God, interpreted dreams, experienced visions, and was delivered from a den of lions. As one of those deported from Judah to Babylon, his faith was put to the test by the rulers Nebuchadnezzar, Belshazzar, Darius, and Cyrus. Chapters 1–6 deal with stories about Daniel and his friends. Chapters 7–12, which are apocalyptic, describe his visions.

These two passages telling about Nebuchadnezzar's dream and the blazing furnace are familiar ones. As you read them make notes about the story line. When you have finished making your notes, respond to this question.

- *How are these stories likely to give courage to those who are facing persecution?*

Daniel 2:24–49, Nebuchadnezzar's Dream

Daniel 3:1–30, The Blazing Furnace

The apocalyptic section of Daniel is more difficult to understand. Some of the characteristics of this type of literature include:

- secret knowledge
- symbolic figures
- a plan and timetable of events
- history divided into time periods.
- symbolic numbers

Read Daniel 7:1–28. See how many of these characteristics you can discover. Write the verse numbers next to the characteristics.

You may be interested in knowing that scholars believe the "little horn" among the ten horns in Daniel 7:8 represents Antiochus IV. Notice that his ultimate destruction is predicted and that the ultimate victory belongs to God's people.

PUTTING IT TOGETHER

This marks the end of the first half of *Kerygma: Discovering the Bible*. Take a few minutes to review where you've been. As you skim through Discoveries 1–15, think about these questions:

- *What is the most exciting thing you have learned about the Bible?*
- *What is the most profound thing you have learned about God?*
- *Of all the people in the Old Testament, whom would you like to know better?*

As you prepare to move on to Discovery 16, the first of the New Testament parts, here is a little background information that helps set the stage. Shortly after the book of Daniel was written, the people of Israel rebelled against the rule of Antiochus IV, who was attempting to impose Greek customs and worship upon the Jews. Led by a family of priests now known as the Maccabees, the people gained a brief period of independence which lasted until 63 B.C., when Jerusalem came under the domination of the Roman Empire.

It was during this time that the Jews began to think more and more about "the day of the Lord" and about the coming of the Messiah, the deliverer promised by God through the prophets long ago. It was into this setting of despair and unrest that Jesus was born.

REFLECTION

1. Reflect upon Israel's expectation for "The Day of the Lord." In what ways was the hope for God's mighty intervention not only a promise but also a threat? How do you think their past as the people of God influenced the way they looked at their future?

2. Review in your mind the ways the promise of God's future was expressed by the prophets. Imagine you were living in Jerusalem in the year 25 B.C. What are you waiting for? What are you hoping for?

NEW
TESTAMENT

Contents

The symbol for *The Good News* is a book, representing the format in which we read the "good news" of Jesus Christ today.

The Good News

THE STORY CONTINUES

Simon Peter answered him, "Lord, to whom can we go? You have the words of eternal life. We have come to believe and know that you are the Holy One of God." John 6:68–69

In the life, death, and resurrection of Jesus of Nazareth, God's promise is fulfilled in a new and marvelous way. Many, through Jesus' life, come to know the power of God's presence. Many, through Jesus' death, come to experience the power of God's love. Many, in Jesus' resurrection, come to discover the power of God's transformation. Many come to share Peter and the disciples' confession of faith: in Jesus Christ there is eternal life.

Initially, this good news of Jesus Christ is shared by eyewitnesses. They proclaim what they have seen and heard: Jesus is alive! They remember the stories Jesus told, the people Jesus healed, and the lives Jesus changed. They testify to the power of God transforming hate to love, fear to hope, anxiety to courage, doubt to faith.

Eventually, the good news of Jesus Christ spreads throughout the world. Letters are sent to proclaim the message and to answer questions of faith. Gospels are written to recall Jesus Christ and to encourage belief in him. Since the letters and Gospels are written in Greek, the common language of the Roman Empire, the events in Palestine can be shared and read by everyone. The dispersion of the Jews throughout the ancient world helps the good news to spread. Within a few decades the twenty-seven books of the New Testament are written, circulated, and collected, although only much later will they be brought together to form the New Testament.

These fifteen Discoveries examine some of the writings that reveal the good news of Jesus Christ.

PREPARING FOR THE SEARCH

Here are some words you need to know as you begin your study of *The Good News*.

Eunuch is the term usually used for a male who has been castrated (either by design or by accident) and therefore is unable to procreate. Eunuchs frequently served as harem guards. Some, like the man from Ethiopia whom Philip met on the road from Jerusalem to Gaza, rose to occupy prominent roles in oriental courts. Eunuchs were forbidden by law to enter "the assembly of the LORD." (Leviticus 23:1)

Galilee, the area where most of Jesus' ministry took place, is located in the northern part of Palestine. The Sea of Galilee and the cities of Nazareth, Capernaum, and Bethsaida were located in this region. Palestine, in the time of Jesus, was divided into three territories: Galilee in the north, Samaria in the middle, and Judea in the south.

Gospel means "good news." The Greek word for "good news" – *evangelion* – became the Latin word *evangelium,* which was then translated into Old English as "godspel" (good story) and finally became "gospel." The word also refers to any one of the first four books of the New Testament that share the good news of Jesus Christ – Matthew, Mark, Luke, and John.

Judea (joo-dee'uh) is the Greco-Latin form of Judah. At times it is thus used to refer to most of Palestine. In the New Testament, however, the term usually indicates the small area around the city of Jerusalem. Herod the Great ruled over this region until approximately 4 B.C. Bethlehem, the location of Jesus' birth, is in Judea. Approximately ten years later Judea was placed under the rule of a Roman procurator.

Synagogue comes from a Greek word that can mean either a gathering of things or an assembly of people. In the New Testament it is a meeting place where Jews gather to study, pray, and worship. As he traveled about all of Galilee, Jesus worshiped and taught in synagogues.

THE SEARCH BEGINS

These passages represent a variety of the types of writing found in the New Testament. Some of the passages will be read again in later Discoveries. As you read them this time, look for the words "good news" or "gospel." Make notes that help you tell where, when, why, how, or by whom the good news was being told. Use these questions to guide your reading:

- *How are the words "good news" or "gospel" used in the passage?*
- *What is the good news that is being told?*

Matthew 4:17–25, Jesus Preaches, Teaches, and Heals

Luke 9:1–6, The Twelve Preach the Gospel

Acts 8:26–39, Philip and the Ethiopian

Romans 1:1–7, Good News

Romans 15:14–21, Paul Writes Boldly

1 Corinthians 15:1–8, The Gospel

Ephesians 6:10–20, God's Armor

2 Timothy 1:3–14, Words of Encouragement

1 Peter 1:3–25, Living Hope

THE SEARCH CONTINUES

In these readings I have questions about...

In these readings I discovered...

FOCUSING THE SEARCH

Like the Old Testament, the New Testament contains stories, sayings, prayers, and hymns that were told, remembered, and retold before they were written down. However, much of the New Testament began as writings. The letters of Paul are examples of these writings.

When the books of the New Testament were put into writing they were written in Greek, which was the common language of many people in the eastern Mediterranean area.

Use the following chart, "The New Testament in Translation," to examine the Greek text and English translation of John 20:30–31.

THE NEW TESTAMENT IN TRANSLATION

John 20:30–31

Today we read the Bible in translations from the original languages. The language of the New Testament is Greek. Greek is read from left to right, just like English.

First, you be the translator. The English translation below the Greek words is from an "interlinear" translation of the Bible. Use this translation to write your own translation at the bottom of this page.

30 Πολλὰ μὲν οὖν καὶ ἄλλα σημεῖα
Many -° therefore and other signs

ἐποίησεν ὁ Ἰησοῦς ἐνώπιον τῶν μαθητῶν,
did - Jesus before the disciples,

ἃ οὐκ ἔστιν γεγραμμένα ἐν τῷ βιβλίῳ
which is(are) not *having been* written in - roll

τούτῳ· **31** ταῦτα δὲ γέγραπται ἵνα
this; but these° has(ve) been written that

πιστεύητε ὅτι Ἰησοῦς ἔστιν ὁ χριστὸς ὁ
ye may believe that Jesus is the Christ the

υἱὸς τοῦ θεοῦ, καὶ ἵνα πιστεύοντες ζωὴν
Son - of God, and that believing life

ἔχητε ἐν τῷ ὀνόματι αὐτοῦ.
ye may have in the name of him.

Second, write down how this passage has been translated in the Bible you use.

PUTTING IT TOGETHER

The twenty-seven books of the New Testament proclaim the good news about Jesus. Included are four books, Matthew, Mark, Luke, and John, that are called Gospels; Acts, a book about the history of the early church; twenty-one letters; and an apocalypse, the Revelation.

Locate in the front of your Bible the page that lists the names of the New Testament books and their abbreviations. On the following chart write these abbreviations beside the names of the books. Next to each abbreviation are the numbers of the Discoveries in this course that focus on that book.

THE NEW TESTAMENT SCRIPTURES

Literature	Book	Abbreviation	Discovery
Gospel	Matthew	_____	16, 17, 18, 19, 20, 21, 22, 29
	Mark	_____	18, 19, 20, 21, 22, 29
	Luke	_____	16, 17, 18, 19, 20, 21, 22
	John	_____	16, 17, 18, 19, 20, 21, 22
History	Acts	_____	16, 23, 24, 25, 26
Letters	Romans	_____	16, 26, 28, 29
	1 Corinthians	_____	16, 26, 27, 29
	2 Corinthians	_____	26, 27
	Galatians	_____	26, 28

Literature	Book	Abbreviation	Discovery
Letters (cont.)	Ephesians	_____	16, 27, 28
	Philippians	_____	30
	Colossians	_____	26, 28
	1 Thessalonians	_____	27, 29
	2 Thessalonians	_____	
	1 Timothy	_____	
	2 Timothy	_____	16, 28
	Titus	_____	
	Philemon	_____	
	Hebrews	_____	
	James	_____	28
	1 Peter	_____	16, 27, 28
	2 Peter	_____	
	1 John	_____	28
	2 John	_____	
	3 John	_____	
	Jude	_____	
Apocalypse	Revelation	_____	29

REFLECTION

1. Reflect upon the good news of Jesus Christ. What is the most fundamental good news you have heard about Jesus Christ? What good news do you have to share with others?

2. In John 20:30–31 John gives his purpose for writing the good news of Jesus Christ: "Now Jesus did many other signs in the presence of his disciples, which are not written in this book. But these are written so that you may come to believe that Jesus is the Messiah, the Son of God, and that through believing you may have life in his name."

"Life" is an important word for John. What do you think about when you think of life? What does it mean to you to have life in the name of Jesus?

The symbol for *The Savior* is the star that guided the wise men to Jesus. (Matthew 2:2)

The Savior

THE STORY CONTINUES

In the time of King Herod, after Jesus was born in Bethlehem of Judea, wise men from the East came to Jerusalem, asking, "Where is the child who has been born king of the Jews? For we observed his star at its rising, and have come to pay him homage." Matthew 2:1–2

Hundreds of years after the last of the prophets, the search for God continues. Some search the Scriptures and some search the stars. When Jesus is born in Bethlehem, he is worshiped by shepherds from nearby fields and by visitors from distant lands – for he is to be the Savior of all: the wealthy and the poor, the innocent and the wise.

Mary and Joseph take the child and flee to Egypt to escape Herod's threats. They return home to Nazareth only when Joseph is told in a dream that it is safe. In God's new deliverance Jesus is brought out of Egypt – just as Moses and the people of Israel were. At the age of twelve Jesus visits the Temple in Jerusalem. Then he is back in Nazareth with his family.

The New Testament accounts of Jesus' life are not biographies; there is much about his life that is untold. Instead, the stories of Jesus are called Gospels, meaning good news. Matthew, Mark, Luke, and John each write a Gospel to tell the "good news" of Jesus of Nazareth. All four include stories about Jesus' life, death, and resurrection. Two, Matthew and Luke, write about his birth and childhood. Since these Gospels are written after Jesus' resurrection, all the stories about him, including the stories of his birth and childhood, are told by people who recognized and experienced Jesus as the risen Christ, the Son of God, the Savior of humanity.

Even though you may already know the story of Jesus, each Gospel is written as though you are asking the question: "Who is Jesus?" The next seven Discoveries provide opportunities to search for answers to that question.

PREPARING FOR THE SEARCH

The definitions of these people, places, and terms will help you prepare to study *The Savior.*

Anna, a devout woman of advanced age who visited the Temple daily, was there the day Mary and Joseph brought Jesus to be dedicated to God. Along with Simeon, she recognized the baby Jesus as the Messiah. (Luke 2:36–38)

Bethlehem, a village about five miles south of Jerusalem on the main highway to Hebron and Egypt, was the birthplace of Jesus. Before Jesus' birth, the importance of Bethlehem centered on the lives of Ruth, Jesse, and David. Bethlehem is the setting for most of Ruth's story. Jesse, David's father, made his home in Bethlehem, and David was anointed king there by Samuel.

Caesar Augustus, first Roman Emperor, ruled from about 27 B.C. to 14 A.D. For purposes of taxation, Caesar Augustus ordered the census (or enrollment) of the Roman Empire that resulted in Mary and Joseph journeying to Bethlehem.

Christ (See Messiah)

Elizabeth, wife of the priest Zechariah, became the mother of John the Baptist in her old age. She was a kinswoman of Mary, mother of Jesus, and was visited by Mary at her home in the hill country of Judea. Elizabeth recognized that Mary's child was to be God's promised Messiah. (Luke 1:5–45)

Emmanuel (or Immanuel), which means "God with us," was the name given by the prophet Isaiah to the child to be born to a young woman. (Isaiah 7:14) Matthew believed that Jesus fulfilled the words of Isaiah, so he quoted the prophet in his Gospel. Jesus is "God with us." (Matthew 1:22–23)

Frankincense and Myrrh were two gifts brought to Jesus by the Wise Men. They were gum resins used to produce incense and perfume. Both were highly prized. Myrrh was also used in embalming.

Gabriel, an angel, was sent as God's messenger to both Daniel the prophet and Zechariah the priest. It was Gabriel who helped Daniel with the meaning of a dream and the interpretation of a vision. (Daniel 8:15–26; 9:20–27) Gabriel announced to Zechariah that he and his wife Elizabeth would be parents of John. (Luke 1:11–22)

Herod the Great, King of Judea, ruled from 37–4 B.C. After the wise men had arrived in Jerusalem to worship the new king of the Jews, Herod felt a further threat to his power and ordered the murder of all the boys in Bethlehem under the age of two. (He had already murdered many rivals to his throne, including two of his sons.) Following Herod's death, three of his own sons divided his kingdom. When Mary, Joseph, and Jesus returned from Egypt, they settled in Galilee where Herod Antipas ruled (4 B.C. – 39 A.D.) rather than Judea, which was under the treacherous rule of Herod Archelaus (4 B.C. – 6 A.D.).

Jesus. The name is a Latin translation of the Greek name Iesous, which is a translation of the Hebrew name Joshua. The meaning in Hebrew is "Yahweh is salvation." Jesus was given his name by God's angel, who said to Joseph, "...you are to name him Jesus, for he will save his people from their sins." (Matthew 1:21)

Joseph, pledged in marriage to Mary, became her husband after an angel of God told him the wonderful news that Jesus, the baby Mary was carrying, was conceived by God in order to save people from their sins. A descendant of the house of David, Joseph journeyed with Mary to Bethlehem at the time of the census, presented Jesus in the Temple for dedication, fled to Egypt to avoid Herod, and returned to Nazareth to live. Joseph does not play an active role during Jesus' ministry, and may have died some time before Jesus' crucifixion and resurrection.

Mary, pledged in marriage to Joseph, became pregnant after God's angel told her the wonderful news that through the power of the Holy Spirit she would conceive and give birth to God's son. The angel named him Jesus, because in him God was to save people from their sins. Mary became the wife of Joseph and together they journeyed to Bethlehem for the census. While there she gave birth to Jesus, who was visited by shepherds from the surrounding fields and wise men from the distant east. Mary probably lived in Nazareth throughout Jesus' ministry. At his crucifixion she was at the cross with the other women. She joined the disciples after Jesus' ascension.

Messiah, a Hebrew word meaning "anointed one," was first used for any person anointed with holy oil – priest, king, or chosen one. Later, by the time of Jesus, the term Messiah had come to designate the one God would anoint to deliver the people and establish the Kingdom. When Jesus came to be known as the Messiah, he was given the title "Christ," the Greek term for "anointed one."

Nazareth, a small village in the region of Galilee, was the home of Joseph, Mary, and Jesus. All the references to Nazareth in the Bible are found in the New Testament, and all are used in connection with Jesus, who is identified nineteen times as "Jesus of Nazareth." Mary was living in Nazareth when she received the announcement from the angel Gabriel, and after Jesus' birth in Bethlehem, Joseph and Mary returned home to Nazareth to live. (Luke 1:26; 2:39–40)

Purification. Forty days after the birth of a male child Jewish mothers underwent the ritual of purification. (Leviticus 12:2–8) A lamb was offered as a sacrifice, or if the parents could not afford a lamb, a pair of pigeons or doves could be substituted. Mary went to the Temple to be purified after the birth of Jesus. Rules about ritual purity were not restricted to childbirth.

Savior is a term that means one who delivers from danger. In the Old Testament the term is used for the judges and other leaders who save the people in times of crisis. It is used especially of God, who delivers Israel from bondage and threats of destruction. In Luke 2:11 the angels announce the birth of Jesus by telling the shepherds that "a Savior, who is the Messiah, the Lord" has been born in Bethlehem.

Simeon, a devout Jew, had been promised by the Holy Spirit that he would see God's Messiah. When Mary and Joseph presented Jesus in the Temple Simeon recognized him at once as the Messiah and knew the promise had been kept. (Luke 2:22–35)

Wise Men, astrologers from the East, unacquainted with the scriptural prophecy of the location of the Messiah's birth, came to worship the child they believed to be the new king of the Jews. They are identified in *Today's English Version* as "men who study the stars," and in the *New International Version* as "Magi," from the Greek root meaning "magic." Traditionally, especially in Christmas carols, they have been called "the Three Kings," although Matthew does not indicate their number.

THE SEARCH BEGINS

The story told in the passages below is a familiar one. However, try to read these texts as if you have never encountered them before. Since each of the writers has a distinctive witness to share, do not blend the passages together, but try to remember which events appear in Matthew, which in Luke, and which in John. As you read, make notes that help you to retell the story of *The Savior.* Use these questions to guide your work:

- *What do the Gospels of Matthew and Luke tell us of Jesus' birth and childhood?*

- *In what ways do the stories of Jesus' birth and childhood anticipate his life and ministry?*

- *What evidence do you find that Jesus was understood as the fulfillment of the promises, prophecies, and hopes expressed in the Hebrew Scriptures?*

Matthew 1:18–25, The Birth of Jesus

Matthew 2:1–12, Eastern Visitors

Matthew 2:13–23, Egypt: Escape and Return

Luke 1:26–56, Jesus' Birth is Announced

Luke 2:1–7, The Birth of Jesus

Luke 2:8–20, The Shepherds Visit Jesus

Luke 2:21–38, Jesus, Simeon, and Anna

Luke 2:39–40, Return to Nazareth

Luke 2:41–52, Jesus in the Temple

John 1:1–18, The Word

THE SEARCH CONTINUES

In these readings I have questions about...

In these readings I discovered...

FOCUSING THE SEARCH

You already know the importance of focusing on what the Bible actually says, not what you think it says or may remember it says. When we retell the story of Jesus' birth, we often integrate elements from Matthew and Luke with ideas from movies, plays, and works of art. Sometimes we add things dimly remembered from childhood.

As you prepared "The Search Begins," you read the accounts of Jesus' birth in Matthew and Luke. Without looking back at your notes or at your Bible, write in your own words the story of the birth as you remember it. Put in as many details as you can.

Now open your Bible to Matthew 1:18–2:12. Underline or mark with a highlighter everything in your story of the birth of Jesus that comes from this passage. Next, check to see if the remaining material comes from Luke 2:1–20. Draw a line through all of the material that is not based on the biblical narratives.

What did you learn from this exercise?

What was Matthew emphasizing?

What was Luke emphasizing?

Why do you think the accounts have different elements?

PUTTING IT TOGETHER

The writers of the New Testament were convinced that Jesus was the fulfillment of the promises, prophecies, and hopes in the Hebrew Scriptures.
Therefore, beginning with the stories of Jesus' birth and continuing through
his life, death, and resurrection, they quoted from those Scriptures to indicate the ways Jesus fulfilled God's promises.

For this exercise you need to use a Bible that contains cross references
either as marginal notes or footnotes. These notes indicate where the same
passage, or a parallel reading, is found in the Bible. Use the following exer-

cise to help you discover how, in the passages you read earlier, the Gospel writers interpreted the Scriptures when they told the stories of Jesus' birth.

First, look up and read the Old Testament passage in the left-hand column. In the cross reference notes for that passage locate the New Testament passage in Matthew, Luke, or John that quotes or refers to this Old Testament "prophecy" and write the book, chapter and verse numbers next to the Old Testament citation. Finally, look up the New Testament reference to see how the prophecy was used by either Matthew, Luke, or John.

Old Testament Passages Quoted or Referred to in the Birth Narratives:	New Testament Passage(s):
Micah 5:2	
Isaiah 7:14	
Isaiah 9:7	

As you read the New Testament, you may note some variation from the words of the Hebrew Scripture. That often occurs because a New Testament writer was quoting from the Greek translation of the Old Testament (the Septuagint), while your Bible is a translation of the Hebrew Old Testament. Sometimes in New Testament cross references you find the notation *LXX* in parentheses. This indicates that the quotation is from the Septuagint.

What did you discover about the ways Matthew, Luke, and John viewed Jesus and his fulfillment of the Old Testament in your search?

In each Discovery continue to look for ways the New Testament writers indicate that Jesus is the fulfillment of the Old Testament prophecies.

REFLECTION

1. Reflect upon the angel's joyful announcement to the shepherds: "Do not be afraid; for see–I am bringing you good news of great joy for all the people: to you is born this day in the city of David a Savior, who is the Messiah, the Lord." (Luke 2:10–11)

What was the "good news of great joy" that caused the shepherds to leave their flocks and go to Bethlehem? What do you mean when you call Jesus your Savior?

2. Ponder some of the opening words of John's Gospel: "But to all who received him, who believed in his name, he gave power to become children of God, who were born, not of blood or of the will of the flesh or the will of man, but of God." (John 1:12)

What do the words "children of God" say to you? What does it mean to you to be born of God? In what ways have you received and believed in Jesus?

The symbol for *The Ministry* is the descending dove, representing the guidance of the Spirit. (Mark 1:10–12)

The Ministry

THE STORY CONTINUES

Now when Jesus came into the district of Caesarea Philippi, he asked his disciples, "Who do people say that the Son of Man is?"… He said to them, "But who do you say that I am?" (Matthew 16:13,15)

For about thirty years Jesus lives in Nazareth with his family. Only one episode from Jesus' life, a visit to Jerusalem at age twelve, is recorded from that period. Around the age of thirty, Jesus begins his public ministry at the Jordan River when he is baptized by John the Baptist. Following an extended time of preparation in the wilderness of Judea, Jesus returns to the synagogue in Nazareth and announces that in his ministry God is inaugurating a glorious new day. God's power anoints Jesus to release captives, restore sight, remove oppression, and proclaim deliverance.

Jesus recruits twelve disciples to share his ministry of preaching, teaching, and healing. The disciples witness God's good news coming true in everything Jesus does. Those held captive by illness and disease are released and made well. Those who are physically and spiritually blind are healed and given sight. Those oppressed by crippling physical and emotional conditions are restored to wholeness.

At a turning point in his ministry, knowing that he must journey to Jerusalem, Jesus questions his disciples about their understanding of all that they have experienced with him, their friend, teacher, and master. Jesus asks them, "But who do you say I am?" In Peter's answer the truth comes out and life is never the same.

PREPARING FOR THE SEARCH

These definitions will help you discover information about *The Ministry* of Jesus.

Andrew, originally one of John the Baptist's disciples, became a disciple of Jesus after John identified Jesus as the "Lamb of God." Along with his brother Peter, whom he brought to Jesus, he was a fisherman living in Capernaum when Jesus called them to follow him. (John 1:35–42; 6:6–9; Matthew 4:18)

Baptism is a symbolic rite of purification with water. In the New Testament baptism is part of the ministry of John the Baptist. After Pentecost it became the rite of initiation into the Christian community. Baptism forms the beginning and end of Jesus' ministry. He was baptized by John the Baptist in the Jordan River, and at his ascension, commissioned his disciples to baptize and make disciples.

Bartholomew, one of the twelve apostles, is little known. He is not mentioned in the Gospel of John, and except for his listing among the twelve in the synoptics, he is not mentioned further in the Bible.

Bethsaida (beth-say' uh-duh) was a fishing village on the northeast shore of the Sea of Galilee near where the Jordan River flows into it. It was in the area where Jesus miraculously fed five thousand people and healed the blind man (Mark 8:22–26). Bethsaida is also identified as the home of three disciples – Philip, Andrew, and Peter. (John 1:44)

Caesarea Philippi (ses-uh-ree' uh fi-lip'i) was a territory in the north of Palestine that was the scene of Peter's confession of faith. "The villages of Caesarea Philippi" (Mark 8:27) were located at the foot of Mount Hermon.

Capernaum (cah-purh' nay-uhm) became Jesus' home after he left Nazareth. Whenever Capernaum is mentioned in the New Testament it is usually in relation to a healing of one of the many people there who sought out Jesus. Capernaum is the setting for the healing of the centurion's servant, a man with an unclean spirit, the government official's son, Peter's mother-in-law, and the paralytic who was lowered through the roof.

Demon is used in the Bible in many different ways, usually describing an evil spirit. These spirits often have names and are conquered by the power of Jesus. In the Gospel of Mark the demons are the first to recognize Jesus. According to the *Harper's Bible Dictionary,* "...demonology was a part of the culture of the New Testament world and should be interpreted and understood against that background."

Devil (See Satan)

Disciple comes from *disciplus,* the Latin word for "learner, pupil." It accurately translates the meaning of the Hebrew and Greek words used in the Scriptures for "pupil." In the New Testament the term "disciple" is used inclusively to refer to any follower of Jesus (male or female), and more narrowly to refer to the twelve Jesus called as disciples. Those disciples who witnessed the resurrection of Jesus and were commissioned by him are also called apostles, and the terms are at times used interchangeably in the New Testament.

The Holy Spirit is the Spirit of God present and active in the creation. In the Old Testament the Spirit inspires prophets and equips judges and kings for leadership. In the New Testament the Spirit is also spoken of as the Spirit of Christ and the Spirit of the Lord. This Spirit is dramatically given to the community at Pentecost. The Spirit provides gifts to build up the church, and guides and empowers the church's mission.

James, son of Zebedee, was a fisherman. He and his brother John joined Jesus as disciples early in his ministry. Jesus nicknamed them "Boanerges," which means "sons of thunder." They were close associates of Jesus and together with Peter were present at the Transfiguration and Jesus' ordeal in the Garden of Gethsemane.

James the Son of Alpheus, accompanied Jesus and the other eleven disciples throughout all of Galilee and Judea. He is sometimes called "James, the younger." Little else is known about him.

John, brother of James, was called to be one of the Twelve while he was fishing. Paul calls John one of the pillars of the Jerusalem church. Although he is often regarded as the author of the Fourth Gospel and other New Testament books, this is not certain.

John the Baptist, son of Zechariah and Elizabeth and cousin of Jesus, was understood by many to be Elijah returned, the forerunner of God's Messiah. After years of seclusion in the desert, John appeared at the Jordan River around 27 A.D. preaching about the coming Kingdom of God and the baptism of the Holy Spirit. John baptized Jesus and, until John was beheaded by Herod, their ministries coincided. Both John the Baptist and Jesus had disciples.

Jordan River, the major river in Israel, was the scene of many of God's mighty acts in Israel's history. Joshua and the people crossed over in triumph to occupy the land. Saul and David both crossed by night to avoid defeat. Elijah and Elisha both crossed over the miraculously divided river. Jesus was baptized in the Jordan River and was never far from it during his ministry.

Judas Iscariot may have been the only disciple from Judea. He held an important position among the Twelve, being treasurer for the group. For reasons that are not clear, Judas betrayed Jesus, selling the information concerning his whereabouts for thirty pieces of silver. He later tried to undo the deed but was unsuccessful. In remorse he hanged himself.

Kingdom of God. When Jesus began to preach and teach, he proclaimed both the arrival and the coming of the Kingdom of God. Jesus' life and teaching demonstrated that God's Kingdom had already arrived – the sick were healed, the dead were raised, the blind were given sight, and sins were forgiven. Jesus' death and resurrection also showed that God's rule is powerful and present. But the Kingdom of God is not yet fully here. Those who believe have a new life now, but in the future all will know the fullness of God's rule.

Mark, known as John Mark in the book of Acts, is traditionally considered to be the author of the second Gospel. He joined Paul and Barnabas on the first missionary journey to Cyprus, but left before its completion. For that reason Paul would not take him on a later journey. Ten years later their differences were reconciled and Mark became Paul's helper in Rome.

Matthew, tax collector at Capernaum, became a disciple upon Jesus' invitation and subsequently wrote one of the Gospels.

Nicodemus, a Pharisee and member of the Sanhedrin (the supreme Jewish council), met Jesus at night, spoke up for him at a meeting of the Sanhedrin, and helped prepare Jesus' body for burial.

Peter, also known as Simon, was a fisherman from Galilee. He and his brother, Andrew, were among the first disciples of Jesus. Scripture portrays Peter as an eager, sometimes stubborn and spontaneous person who occasionally acted before he thought. Nevertheless, he was a leader among those who followed Jesus. After Jesus' death, Peter had a prominent role in leading the church in Jerusalem. He preached at Pentecost, had a revelation at Joppa to preach to non-Jews, and probably passed on his gospel message to Mark. Tradition has it that he was killed in Rome, crucified upside down.

Pharisees, a word which may mean "separated ones," was the name of a major Jewish group at the time of Jesus. Other important groups were the Sadducees, the Essenes, and the Zealots. The Pharisees began to come into prominence in the second century B.C., when there was a concern to follow the Jewish Law more strictly. They developed detailed rulings about the observance of the Law in everyday life. The largest Jewish group by Jesus' day, they were perhaps 6,000 strong. Jesus frequently challenged their strict interpretation of the Law as being legalistic and self-righteous. Nicodemus and Paul were both Pharisees.

Philip was called to be one of Jesus' disciples, as were two others from his home in Bethsaida, Andrew and Peter. In the Gospel of John, the author portrays Philip as one who never fully understands Jesus' ministry, yet he brings Nathaniel to meet Jesus. He also provides Jesus the opportunity to perform a miracle and express further truth. (Matthew 10:3; John 1:43–46)

Rabbi, a Hebrew word originally meaning "my teacher, my master," is the term of respect given to a spiritual leader. Jesus was called "rabbi," which by his time meant simply "master," as did "rabboni."

Sabbath. The Jewish day of worship begins at sundown on Friday and ends at sundown on Saturday, reflecting God's day of rest recorded in Genesis 2:1–3. By the time of Jesus over three hundred "laws" had been written, controlling the actions of Jews on the Sabbath. Jesus was often accused by the Pharisees of ignoring the law because he healed people on the Sabbath.

Satan. When used without the definite article, the Hebrew word is translated as "adversary" or "accuser." When the article is used in the Hebrew, the translation is a proper name – Satan. The Greek word for "satan" is *diabolos* – translated "devil." Satan, the tempter, the force of evil, is the adversary of

God. Jesus was tempted by Satan; Judas carried out Satan's work; and Jesus' healings proved superior to Satan's power. In the resurrection of Jesus, God defeated Satan. Even though Satan is still God's adversary, God's victory will be total at the end of the age.

Scribes were people who copied and interpreted the Law. Ezra is the Old Testament prototype of the group referred to by this term in the New Testament. Jesus often spoke of "the scribes and the Pharisees" and it may be that the scribes were the scholarly representatives of this well-known sect.

Scroll. Scripture and other important works were written on long strips of parchment, leather, or papyrus and rolled into scrolls. The rods placed at the ends of these strips made it possible to roll and unroll a manuscript to the location of a passage to be read.

Sea of Galilee is just one of the names for the scene of so many episodes and teachings in Jesus' life. An earlier name for the Sea of Galilee was the Lake of Chinnereth, named for a nearby town. The word Chinnereth means "lyre," and referred either to the shape of the town or the shape of the lake. Other names in the New Testament that refer to the same body of water are Lake Gennesaret (Luke 5:1) and the Sea of Tiberias. (John 6:1)

Simon, sometimes identified as "the Zealot" or "the Canaanean," was one of the Twelve. He may have been a member of the Zealot party, whose aim was to drive the Romans out of their nation. The Zealots' attitude towards the Romans could be stated, "The only good Roman is a dead Roman."

Son of God, a title infrequently used in the Old Testament to refer to the nation of Israel, the king, or the angels, is used in the New Testament to refer to God's Messiah, Jesus of Nazareth. The title is used forty-five times in the New Testament, all but once in relation to Jesus.

Son of Man was the title Jesus most often used to speak of himself. Jesus no doubt chose this title with its many interpretations in order to avoid taking on other titles forced upon him by both friends and enemies. In the Gospels, Jesus calls himself the Son of Man seventy-eight times. In the Old Testament the term is frequently used by Ezekiel and Daniel.

Thaddaeus, whose name means "large hearted" in Greek or "courageous" in Hebrew, is listed as one of Jesus' twelve apostles in Matthew and Mark.

Thomas, often referred to as "doubting Thomas" because of his need for physical proof that the resurrected Jesus was indeed alive, was one of the original twelve disciples. In John's Gospel he is called "Didymus," meaning twin. On one occasion he evidenced great courage, urging the disciples to accompany Jesus to Jerusalem, even if it would lead to death. (John 11:16)

The Twelve. Twelve is a significant number in the Bible. There are twelve divisions in the Hebrew lunar year, twelve tribes, and twelve disciples. As a name, "The Twelve," is an alternative term for Jesus' disciples. The number is an important image in the New Testament. (See Revelation 12:1; 21:12–14; 22:2.)

THE SEARCH BEGINS

In these passages there is more to discover about Jesus and his ministry. Take careful notes to be able to retell the story of *The Ministry*. Consider these questions as you read:

- *How did Jesus begin his ministry?*

- *Where did Jesus' ministry take place? What area did he cover?*

- *What did Jesus do that captured the attention of the people?*

- *How would you characterize the relationship between Jesus and his disciples?*

Mark 1:1–20, The Good News Begins

Matthew 3:13–4:17, Jesus' Baptism and Temptation

Luke 4:14–30, Jesus Fulfills Scripture

Mark 1:21–39, Jesus Heals the People

John 6:1–14, Jesus Feeds Five Thousand

Matthew 16:13–20, Who Do You Say I Am?

John 3:1–21, Jesus and Nicodemus

THE SEARCH CONTINUES

In these readings I have questions about...

In these readings I discovered...

FOCUSING THE SEARCH

It is important to recognize the individual characteristics of each of the twenty-seven books in the New Testament, as well as the characteristics they share in common. This search to discover the names of Jesus' disciples discloses one instance of similarities and differences among the four Gospels.

All the Gospels tell the story of Jesus Christ. Matthew, Mark, and Luke are called the "Synoptic Gospels" because they see and report events as if with the same eye (syn-optic). The Gospel of John sees and reports Jesus' life differently from the other three. To discover the names of Jesus' disciples we can read either Matthew, Mark, Luke, or John. Even though many of the names are shared in common, the lists reveal individual differences. Use this chart to see what you can discover by comparing the four passages.

JESUS' DISCIPLES

Jesus' disciples are named in various places in the New Testament. Write down the names of the disciples given in each of the following passages. What do you discover by comparing the lists?

Matthew 10:1–4	Mark 3:13–19	Luke 6:12–16	John 1:35–50
_____	_____	_____	_____
_____	_____	_____	_____
_____	_____	_____	_____
_____	_____	_____	_____
_____	_____	_____	_____
_____	_____	_____	_____
_____	_____	_____	_____
_____	_____	_____	_____
_____	_____	_____	_____
_____	_____	_____	_____
_____	_____	_____	_____

PUTTING IT TOGETHER

It is helpful to be able to identify and locate the major settings of Jesus' life in order to get a picture of the limited geographic area of his ministry. His early ministry centered in Galilee, in the north; the later ministry in Judah, to the south.

First, locate the map of "Palestine in the Time of Jesus" on page 190 and mark with a colored dot the following towns and places:

Bethsaida, Caesarea Philippi, Capernaum, Galilee, Jerusalem, Jordan River, Judea, Lake Galilee (also known as the Sea of Galilee), Nazareth

Next, use the map to answer these questions:

    a. What is the length of the Jordan River? _____

    b. How far is it from:

        Nazareth to Jerusalem? _____

        Capernaum to Nazareth?_____

        Caesarea Philippi to Capernaum?_____

        Bethsaida to the southern tip of Lake Galilee? _____

    c. Galilee is approximately _____ square miles or kilometers?

    d. How long do you think it would take you to walk from:

        Nazareth to Jerusalem? _____

        Capernaum to Nazareth?_____

        Caesarea Philippi to Capernaum?_____

    e. How long might it take to row from Bethsaida to Tiberias? _____

    f. What did you discover about the area of Palestine?

REFLECTION

    1. Reflect upon Jesus' invitation to Peter and Andrew, "Follow me..." What thoughts and feelings do you think the disciples had about Jesus' call to discipleship?

Jesus also invites you to be his disciple, and he says to you, "Follow me." How do you respond? What thoughts and feelings do you have?

2. Consider Jesus' question to his disciples, "Who do you say I am?" What do you think some of the disciples may have answered?

Jesus asks you, "Who do you say I am?" What thoughts and feelings do you have as you consider your answer?

Palestine in the Time of Jesus

© United Bible Societies, 1976

The symbol for *The Teachings* is Jesus standing on a hillside, representing the Sermon on the Mount. (Matthew 5:1–7:29)

DISCOVERY 19

The Teachings

THE STORY CONTINUES

Just then a lawyer stood up to test Jesus. "Teacher," he said, "what must I do to inherit eternal life?" Luke 10:25

Jesus teaches at every opportunity, especially when someone asks him a question. Everyone he teaches – the crowds, his disciples, and the authorities – ask him questions. The answers are likely to be more challenging than they expect. On one occasion, Jesus answers a lawyer's question, but the lawyer is not satisfied, so he asks still another question. Jesus responds with a story that begins, "A man was going down from Jerusalem to Jericho...," as if to say, "You figure it out."

Many people gather around Jesus and follow him from village to village wanting to know more about him, about God, and about themselves. Some people enthusiastically receive his teachings. To some, his teachings either sound too unrealistic or simply raise more questions. Even his closest disciples are slow to understand. It is easy to believe that sometimes they want to ask, "Jesus, why don't you say what you mean?" To others his teachings sound dangerous and unsettling. Perhaps getting his message across will take more than teaching.

Other people, often the religious leaders, ask questions of Jesus to start arguments, to try to trip him, to provoke conflict, or to prove themselves superior. Jesus often answers them with stories; some they fail to understand, others they understand all too well. But Jesus is a master teacher. He knows that good teaching means involving the learner in making a personal discovery by finding the connections between the story and real life.

Jesus uses many teaching methods: parables, healings, actions, and sermons. He sees in the objects and situations around him endless opportunities to proclaim God's call to righteous living and express his own mission to save the lost. Jesus knows that those who discover the answers to their deepest questions will be as joyful as someone who finds what was lost.

PREPARING FOR THE SEARCH

The definitions for these names and terms are important in *The Teachings*.

Gentile is the term used for all the nations and peoples who are not Jews. There were sharp separations between Jews and Gentiles on religious and political matters. The early church was transformed when Gentiles were welcomed and evangelized, and the distinctions between Jew and Gentile diminished.

Jericho is a city with an amazing history. At least three different sites were occupied over the centuries, beginning perhaps 11,000 years ago. In Jesus' day, Jericho was the winter capital of the kingdom and a city of great wealth and great poverty. While passing through Jericho, Jesus healed the blind beggar, Bartimaeus, and enjoyed the hospitality of the wealthy Zacchaeus.

Kingdom of Heaven (See Kingdom of God in Discovery 18).

Parable. A parable is a method of teaching in which a religious truth is made clear through the use of an analogy taken from everyday life. A parable shares the features of a simile or a metaphor, yet a parable generally is longer and involves the listener in finishing the story and making a decision. Jesus used parables extensively so that his listeners would remember both the story and the point. He wanted people to think things through for themselves.

Samaritan was originally the name given to an inhabitant of the district of Samaria in Northern Israel. During the Assyrian conquest in 721 B.C., many of the Israelites of Samaria were carried off to Assyria, and the area was partially repopulated by people from lands outside Palestine. Although they brought along their own gods and idols, they soon adopted many Jewish beliefs and customs. Following the period of the Babylonian exile and the rebuilding of Jerusalem, the Jews became increasingly exclusive and they and the Samaritans became more separated. While they shared a common heritage, differences in theology and traditions created conflict. By the time of Jesus, the term Samaritan was used to identify members of a particular ethno-religious community based in the area around Mt. Gerizim. Jesus ministered to the Samaritans and many became Christian converts in the early church.

Scriptures is the word the writers of the New Testament used to refer to the sacred writings of the Hebrews. Generally, when the term "the Scriptures" is used, it refers to any of the books of the Law, History, Prophecy, and Psalms.

When "the Scripture" is used, it refers to the entire collection, understood as one book.

Sermon on the Mount is the name given to a collection of sayings of Jesus recorded in Matthew 5–7. These difficult ethical teachings demand that people examine their motives as well as their actions in light of the arrival of God's Kingdom.

Talent. According to a footnote in the *New Revised Standard Version,* "a talent was worth more than fifteen years' wages of a laborer."

Tax Collectors, or publicans, as they were often called, were considered nothing more than extortioners. Those who actually collected the taxes worked for wealthy Romans who had purchased the rights to gather these revenues. Although a specific sum was levied by Rome, there was no law that limited the amount that could be collected. Therefore, publicans and tax collectors often became very rich, while the common folk fell further and further into debt.

Tyre and Sidon, two Phoenician seaports that had enjoyed a thriving economy during the days of King David and King Solomon, were visited by Jesus during his ministry. They were also visited by Paul during his missionary journeys. (Matthew 15:21; Luke 6:17)

THE SEARCH BEGINS

The passages listed below contain some of the most famous teachings of Jesus. As you read them make notes to help you recall and retell the major points of *The Teachings*. Indicate if the method of teaching being used is an example of storytelling, parable, personal action, or sermon. These questions can help guide your reading:

- *In what ways were the teachings of Jesus memorable?*
- *How did people respond to Jesus' teachings?*
- *What were some of the "unexpected" things Jesus said?*

Matthew 5:1–20, Basics for Living

Matthew 6:5–15, Jesus Teaches about Prayer

Matthew 25:14–30, Parable of the Three Servants

Mark 10:17–31, The Rich Man

Mark 12:28–34, The Great Commandment

19   194

Luke 10:25–37, The Good Samaritan

Luke 15:1–32, The Lost: Sheep, Coin, Son

John 4:5–30, Jesus and the Samaritan Woman

John 10:1–18, Jesus, the Good Shepherd

THE SEARCH CONTINUES

In these readings I have questions about...

In these readings I discovered...

FOCUSING THE SEARCH

Jesus not only taught about prayer, he prayed. The disciples learned to pray by observing Jesus at prayer and following his example. In the same manner, Jesus teaches us to pray. Use the exercise "Jesus Prays" to discover what you can learn about prayer from looking at both Jesus' prayer life and Jesus' prayers.

JESUS PRAYS

As we observe Jesus' life of prayer and his attitude toward prayer, we are taught to pray. Read these selections from the Gospels and answer the following questions:

Matthew 6:5–6	Matthew 21:22	Mark 1:35
Mark 11:24–25	Mark 14:22	Luke 5:15–16
Luke 6:27–28	Luke 11:1–4	Luke 19:45–46

How did Jesus address God?

When did Jesus pray?

What were the settings for Jesus' prayers?

What did Jesus teach about prayer?

PUTTING IT TOGETHER

Jesus taught using "picture language," just as the prophets and teachers in Israel had done before him. Through the use of picturesque stories and sayings Jesus engaged the imaginations of his listeners and left indelible images in their minds. When you read Jesus' words what do you see?

Use your imagination. Review one or more of these passages:

Matthew 5:14–16, Light of the World

Matthew 6:5–6, Teaching about Prayer

Luke 15:1–7, The Lost Sheep

Luke 15:8–10, The Lost Coin

John 10:1–18, The Good Shepherd

Then complete this sentence, either visually (by drawing a picture) or verbally (by writing a description).

When I read about Jesus' story of _____ I see:

REFLECTION

1. Reflect upon Jesus' words in his Sermon on the Mount: "Blessed are the pure in heart, for they will see God."

   What does purity of heart mean to you? What do you think Jesus meant by "seeing God?" What does Jesus say to you in these words?

2. Consider the two sons in the story of "The Good Father" (sometimes called "The Lost Son"), Luke 15:11–32. Which son do you resemble most? If you were the older, obedient son, how would you have responded to the father's enthusiastic reception of your brother?

The symbol for *The Kingdom* is a grain of wheat, representing the seed sown by the sower. (Mark 4:1–20)

The Kingdom

THE STORY CONTINUES

At that time the disciples came to Jesus and asked, "Who is the greatest in the kingdom of heaven?"
Matthew 18:1

Jesus preaches and teaches about the Kingdom of God in everything he says and does, yet his message is difficult to understand. In response to the disciples' misguided question, Jesus embraces and sets a child in the center of their group as if to say that the answer should be clear. In teaching his disciples to pray, Jesus instructs them to pray "your kingdom come."

Jesus' challenge is to transform the common understanding of a kingdom in order to help people anticipate, welcome, and respond to God's coming Kingdom. For whenever Jesus talks about the Kingdom of God, those in the crowds picture another kingdom in their minds. They think back to the majestic kingdom of their ancestors, King David and King Solomon, and imagine glory, wealth, and power. They also think about the might of the Roman Empire, and other rival kingdoms.

It is difficult to put the fullness of God's Kingdom into words. Jesus teaches about the Kingdom of God by making comparisons with objects that people see, and to situations that people experience, saying "the Kingdom of God is like..." These sayings and parables help put the Kingdom of God into pictures so people can gain a new awareness of its meaning.

Jesus further clarifies the meaning of the Kingdom of God in healing, praying, touching, forgiving, and preaching, yet his message is only partly understood. Even Pilate, at Jesus' trial, interrogates him about his kingdom. It seems that Jesus' efforts to transform people's perception from an earthly kingdom to an understanding of God's Kingdom are not complete or effective. Preaching and teaching are not enough. God will have to act in a new way.

PREPARING FOR THE SEARCH

In reading the passages selected for *The Kingdom,* these words are important.

Leaven is a fermenting agent similar to yeast. An unbaked portion of a previous batch of bread is added to the fresh ingredients to make the dough rise. In the Bible leaven sometimes represents evil (Mark 8:15); at other times, as in the Parable of the Leaven, it represents growth. (Matthew 13:33)

Mustard Seed. In the Parable of the Mustard Seed (Matthew 13:31,32), Jesus is quoted as saying that the mustard seed is "...the smallest of all the seeds..." Yet it develops into a tree-like shrub. This hyperbole emphasizes that from small beginnings God's Kingdom will grow.

THE SEARCH BEGINS

The word "kingdom" occurs in each of the following passages. Sometimes it is part of the phrases "Kingdom of God" or "Kingdom of Heaven." At other times it is used without those additional words, but the intent is the same. Take notes that help you retell the story of *The Kingdom.* These questions can guide your reading and note taking:

- *What are some ways Jesus described The Kingdom?*

- *How did Jesus attempt to transform the people's understanding of kingdom?*

- *When/where/what is The Kingdom?*

Matthew 9:35–38, Good News of the Kingdom

Matthew 13:31–33, 44–52, Parables of the Kingdom

Matthew 18:1–5, Who's the Greatest?

Mark 4:1–20, The Parable of the Sower

Mark 10:13–16, Jesus and the Children

Mark 15:1–15, Jesus before Pilate

Luke 10:1–12, Jesus Sends His Followers

Luke 11:1–13, Your Kingdom Come

Luke 13:22–30, The Narrow Door

Luke 14:15–24, Parable of a Dinner

THE SEARCH CONTINUES

In these readings I have questions about...

In these readings I discovered...

FOCUSING THE SEARCH

Those who read the Gospels are sometimes surprised when they discover the same event or story being told in different ways. In *Interpretation: A Guide to Understanding the Bible Today* (The Kerygma Program, 1985), Richard Rohrbaugh says, "As we turn to the Bible, it is important to remember that much of what is in the Scriptures began as oral communication. Very few persons in biblical times could read, and most of what was passed along had to be shared orally and remembered...Oral communication is, however, more fluid than written. Stories, for example, are difficult to retell in exactly the same way...Jesus' parables were, above all, oral communication. They were meant to be remembered, but the situations in which they were shared shaped how they were understood...Each retelling of the story was an occasion for transmitting what had been heard before and for allowing it to be heard and remembered in a new setting."

In "The Search Begins" you read the Parable of the Sower as told in Mark. The same parable is also recounted in Matthew and Luke. As you might suspect, each tells the story in a slightly different way. Compare these passages from Matthew and Luke. Underline all of the words and phrases that are the same or similar in both.

Mark 4:1–9

Again he began to teach beside the sea. Such a very large crowd gathered around him that he got into a boat on the sea and sat there, while the whole crowd was beside the sea on the land. He began to teach them many things in parables, and in his teaching he said to them: "Listen! A sower went out to sow. And as he sowed, some seed fell on the path, the birds came and ate it up. Other seed fell on rocky ground, where it did not have much soil, and it sprang up quickly, since it had no depth of soil. And when the sun rose, it was scorched; and since it had no root, it withered away. Other seed fell among thorns, and the thorns grew up and choked it, and it yielded no grain. Other seed fell into good soil and brought forth grain, growing up and increasing and yielding thirty and sixty and a hundredfold." And he said, "Let anyone with ears to hear listen!"

Luke 8:4–8

When a great crowd gathered and people from town after town came to him, he said in a parable: "A sower went out to sow his seed; and as he sowed, some fell on the path and was trampled on, and the birds of the air ate it up. Some fell on the rock; and as it grew up, it withered for lack of moisture. Some fell among thorns and the thorns grew with it and choked it. Some fell into good soil, and when it grew, it produced a hundredfold." As he said this, he called out, "Let anyone with ears to hear listen!"

What did you discover from this exercise?

On another sheet of paper, write the Parable of the Sower in your own words without looking back at the passages above.

PUTTING IT TOGETHER

Throughout his life and ministry Jesus is known by many names and is addressed by many titles. One popular title given to him, "Lord," indicates his rule and his Kingdom. Read the passages below to discover some of the most frequently used names of Jesus. Write the names you find on the lines next to the passages.

NAMES AND TITLES FOR JESUS

Matthew 14:33 _____

Matthew 16:16 _____

Matthew 26:49 _____

Mark 1:24 _____

Mark 2:10 _____

Luke 2:11 _____

Luke 11:1 _____

Luke 18:18 _____

John 1:1, 14 _____

John 1:29 _____

John 1:41 _____

John 10:11 _____

John 20:16 _____

REFLECTION

1. Jesus told his followers, "...do not worry, saying 'What will we eat?' or 'What will we drink?' or 'What will we wear?' But strive first for the kingdom of God and his righteousness, and all these things will given to you as well." (Matthew 6:31, 33)

What worries keep you from striving for the Kingdom of God?

2. Think about Jesus' Parable of the Sower, Mark 4:1–20. What may have prompted Jesus to tell this parable? What seems to be the most important: the seed, the soil, or the growth? What does the parable say to you about sharing your faith in Jesus with others?

The symbol for *The Crucifixion* is the crown of thorns the soldiers put on Jesus before his death. (Matthew 27:29)

The Crucifixion

THE STORY CONTINUES

...Jesus said, "Truly I tell you, one of you will betray me, one who is eating with me." They began to be distressed and to say to him one after another, "Surely, not I?" Mark 14:18–19

Jesus' decision to journey to Jerusalem for the festival of Passover sets in motion events that will complete his earthly ministry. He enters the city to the wild acclaim of the crowds that continue to gather all week to hear him preach and teach in the Temple courtyards.

Later that week, Jesus celebrates Passover with his disciples and transforms a meal that remembers God's ancient deliverance in the exodus into a meal that celebrates God's new deliverance. "Do this in remembrance of me," he says. Jesus' expectation of betrayal shocks his disciples, and the agitated question circles the table, "Surely not I?" Judas departs. What follows cannot be undone.

After the meal, Jesus and his disciples go to the Garden of Gethsemane. While the disciples sleep, Jesus prays, "My Father, if this cannot pass unless I drink it, your will be done." (Matthew 26:42) In this setting, without the help of the crowds or his disciples, Jesus is arrested. As a prisoner he is examined and mocked. Even Pilate wants to know, "Are you the King of the Jews?" But Jesus does not answer this question directly. Pilate is left to answer the question for himself.

PREPARING FOR THE SEARCH

These names and terms are important ones associated with *The Crucifixion.*

Barabbas (buh-rab'uhs), a robber and a rebel, was already a prisoner when Jesus was arrested. Pilate, the Roman Governor, followed a custom of releasing one prisoner on a feast day and asked the crowd to decide which of the two prisoners would be freed. Encouraged by the chief priests and the elders, the crowd yelled for Barabbas to be freed and Jesus to be crucified. (John 18:38b-40)

Bethany, two miles east of Jerusalem, was Jesus' headquarters during his final week in Jerusalem. Here Jesus raised Lazarus from the dead (John 11:44), visited with Mary and Martha (Luke 10:38–42), had supper with Simon the Leper (Mark 14:3–9), and departed from his disciples after his resurrection. (Luke 24:50–51)

Bethpage was a small village, probably located between Jerusalem and Bethany and close to or on the Mount of Olives. Jesus sent two of his disciples there to fetch the colt for his ride into the city.

Caiaphas, high priest in Jerusalem from 18–36 A.D., was responsible for having Jesus arrested, charging him with blasphemy, finding him guilty, and sending him to Pilate for sentencing. He was joined in this by his father-in-law Annas, also a high priest. Caiaphas later persecuted the early Christians, especially Peter and John.

Crucifixion. In the time of Jesus the Romans used crucifixion as a punishment for many different crimes, including thievery and rebellion against Roman rule. Death by this means could take several days and was brought about by the effects of thirst, exposure, exhaustion, and the scourging before being placed on the cross.

Gethsemane (geth-sem' ah-nee), a garden on the Mount of Olives outside the walls of Jerusalem, is the site of Jesus' prayers following the meal with his disciples in the Upper Room. Mark and Matthew identify the place as Gethsemane; Luke writes that it was "the place" on the Mount of Olives where Jesus usually prayed; and John is the one who describes it as a garden. The name "Gethsemane" is a Greek word taken from the Aramaic word for "oil press," indicating the site of an olive grove and olive press.

Golgotha (gahl' guh-thuh), site of Jesus' death, was located outside the walls of Jerusalem. The origin of its name is uncertain. The basic word means "skull." In Hebrew the word is "Golgotha," in Greek it is "Cranium," and in Latin it is *calvaria,* from which our word "Calvary" is taken.

Joseph of Arimathea was a member of the Sanhedrin (the highest ruling council of the Jews). Joseph supplied the tomb in which Jesus was buried, indicating that he was an admirer, if not a follower, of Jesus. Legend has it that he became a missionary and went to England.

Mount of Olives, a hill just east across the Kidron Valley from Jerusalem, was a major location for many of the crucial events of Jesus' last week. Jesus rode into Jerusalem from the Mount of Olives; he wept over the city from its summit; he journeyed back and forth to Bethany through the groves of olive trees; he prayed in the Garden of Gethsemane; he ascended into heaven from its summit.

Pilate was Roman governor in Judea from A.D. 26–36. His term spanned the activity of John the Baptist and the ministry of Jesus. Pilate was not well liked by the Jews. He permitted Roman soldiers to carry likenesses of the emperor into Jerusalem, causing the citizens to protest his lack of sensitivity to their religious beliefs. During the trial of Jesus, Pilate washed his hands, claiming that Jesus' death was not his responsibility. (Matthew 27:24)

The Temple of Jesus' day was actually the third construction upon the sacred site. The First Temple, created by King Solomon, stood for 350 years until it was destroyed by the Babylonians in 586 B.C. The Second Temple, erected by Zerubbabel, was built following the return of the exiles about 515 B.C. and stood for 400 years. The Temple Jesus knew, the Temple of Herod, had been extensively restored and enlarged in 20 B.C. It existed for just 90 years before being destroyed by the Romans in 70 A.D. In the Temple court-yard merchants made a living exchanging Gentile coins for Jewish money, which could be used to purchase birds and animals for sacrifice. Jesus drove these entrepreneurs from the Temple, saying that they had made it a "den of robbers."

THE SEARCH BEGINS

As you read the passages listed below, you will discover the events that took place during Jesus' last week of ministry. Take notes to help you understand the growing tension that surrounded Jesus during this time. These questions can guide your reading:

  - *How did the mood change from the day of Jesus' triumphal entry until his crucifixion six days later?*

  - *How did the disciples interpret the events that were occurring?*

  - *What are some words you would use to describe the emotions of Jesus, the disciples, the Jewish religious leaders, and the people during these days?*

Mark 11:1–11, Jesus Enters Jerusalem

Mark 11:15–19, Jesus Drives the Money Changers from the Temple

Mark 14:12–26, Jesus Shares the Passover Meal

Mark 14:32–42, Jesus Prays in Gethsemane

Mark 14:43–51, Jesus is Arrested

Mark 14:53–65, Jesus is Taken before the Sanhedrin

Mark 15:1–15, Jesus is Taken before Pilate

Mark 15:16–41, Jesus is Crucified

Mark 15:42–47, Jesus is Buried

THE SEARCH CONTINUES

In these readings I have questions about...

In these readings I discovered...

FOCUSING THE SEARCH

In this exercise you are going to focus on *one* of the events of Jesus' final week in Jerusalem. From the list below select an event about which you would like to know more.

Jesus enters Jerusalem. Mark 11:1–11

Jesus drives the money changers from the Temple. Mark 11:15–19

Jesus shares the Passover meal. Mark 14:12–26

Jesus prays in Gethsemane. Mark 14:32–42

Jesus is arrested. Mark 14:43–51

Jesus is taken before the Sanhedrin. Mark 14:53–65

Jesus is taken before Pilate. Mark 15:1–15

Jesus is crucified. Mark 15:16–41

Jesus is buried. Mark 15:42–47

Read the account in Mark. Then using the cross reference notes in your Bible, read the parallel passages in the other Gospels to gather additional information about the location, time of day, people who are present, mood, etc. Imagine you are commissioning an artist to capture the scene. Using this form as a guide, indicate what you want to have included in the "painting."

Title:

Time of day:

Prominent people present:

Other people in the background:

General expressions on their faces:

Location of the event:

Action taking place:

Overall mood of the scene:

The most important element:

What was Luke emphasizing?

Why do you think the accounts have different elements?

If you can find a reproduction of a painting of this event, check to see if the artist included the things you thought were the most important. Bring the picture to share with the group.

PUTTING IT TOGETHER

All four Gospels tell the story of Jesus' crucifixion. However, each writer provides different details and information. By reading all four accounts you gain a clearer picture of the events of Good Friday. One way to bring together the various pictures of Jesus' crucifixion is to gather the seven last sayings of Jesus from the cross as recorded by Matthew, Mark, Luke, and John. Read the passages below and write the words of Jesus on the lines provided.

Matthew 27:46 _____

Mark 15:34 _____

Luke 23:34 _____

Luke 23:43 _____

Luke 23:46 _____

John 19:26–27 _____

John 19:28 _____

John 19:30 _____

Which of these seven last "words" did you find the most surprising? Why?

REFLECTION

1. Read Psalm 22. Although this psalm reflects Israel's faith in times of distress, in many ways its words recall the distress Jesus may have been feeling during Holy Week. He quoted the first verse of this psalm from the cross. What do Jesus' words from the cross mean to you? In what ways does being familiar with the entire psalm help you understand why Jesus quoted it?

2. At the foot of Jesus' cross the centurion proclaimed, "Truly this man was God's Son!" (Matthew 27:54) What does it mean to call Jesus "God's Son?"

What do you think convinced the centurion of that fact? What has convinced you?

The symbol for *The Resurrection* is the stone rolled away from Jesus' tomb. (Luke 24:2)

The Resurrection

THE STORY CONTINUES

...The men said to them, "Why do you look for the living among the dead? He is not here, but has risen. Remember how he told you, while he was still in Galilee, that the Son of Man must be handed over to sinners, and be crucified, and on the third day rise again." Luke 24:5b-7

Early on the first day of the week, three days after his death, the women who had come from Galilee and had prepared Jesus' body after the crucifixion, go to the tomb. They find it open and empty, guarded by two men in dazzling apparel. The guardians of the tomb ask them why they expect to find him there, when he is alive. They return to the gathered disciples, and report what they have seen and heard. He is alive! The day is filled with the presence of the risen Christ. Jesus appears to Peter, and to two disciples walking to Emmaus. He is alive! Each of the disciples sees Jesus, and each one has a story to tell that expresses a personal experience with Jesus, the risen Lord. It is not a time for questions; it is a time for wonder and joy.

Later it is Jesus' turn to ask questions. Jesus asks Peter the same question, "Do you love me?" three times and offers Peter three directives to take the place of the three earlier denials. Peter answers, "Yes, Lord, you know that I love you."

In the days, months, years, and centuries to follow, both questions continue to be addressed to Jesus' followers: "Whom are you looking for?" and "Do you love me?"

PREPARING FOR THE SEARCH

The location and names below are associated with *The Resurrection*.

Emmaus (eh-may'uhs), a village probably located about seven miles from Jerusalem, is mentioned only once in the Bible. It was the destination of two of Jesus' followers on the day of his resurrection. One of the disciples was identified as Cleopas, his only mention in the Bible. Jesus joined them on the road and opened their hearts to the Scriptures as they talked. In Emmaus he broke bread with them. Only then did they recognize him.

Joanna, the wife of one of Herod's officials, was healed by Jesus, and out of gratitude contributed to the support of Jesus and his disciples. She was among the women who went to Jesus' tomb and experienced the joy of the resurrection proclamation.

Mary, the mother of James, one of six Marys mentioned in the New Testament, was present at Jesus' crucifixion and was also with the women who went to the tomb to anoint Jesus' body. She may be the same as "the other Mary" and "Mary, wife of Cleopas" named in the Gospels.

Mary Magdalene, one of Jesus' most faithful disciples, was from Magdala, a town on the Sea of Galilee. Early in his ministry Jesus had healed her, and she remained his devoted follower. Mary Magdalene was at Jesus' crucifixion, his burial, and went to anoint his body. In the Gospel of Mark she is identified as the first person to see the risen Lord.

Salome, mother of James and John, was one who cared for Jesus and the disciples during their ministry in Galilee. She witnessed Jesus' crucifixion and went with the women to anoint his body on the morning of his resurrection.

THE SEARCH BEGINS

These passages contain the testimonies of those who experienced *The Resurrection* of Jesus. The notes that you make will help you retell the story. Keep these questions in mind:

- *How did the disciples experience and understand Jesus' resurrection?*

- *What convinced Jesus' followers that he was alive?*

- *What does the resurrection of Jesus mean to you?*

Matthew 28:1–10, The Resurrection of Jesus

Mark 16:1–8, The Resurrection of Jesus

Luke 24:1–12, The Resurrection of Jesus

John 20:1–18, The Resurrection of Jesus

Matthew 28:11–15, The Guards' Report

Luke 24:13–35, The Walk to Emmaus

Luke 24: 36–53, Jesus Commissions His Disciples

John 20:19–21:25, Appearances of Jesus

THE SEARCH CONTINUES

In these readings I have questions about...

In these readings I discovered...

FOCUSING THE SEARCH

Imagine the impact the resurrection of Jesus had on those who experienced it. While some believed instantly, others took longer. A few even wanted "proof," and some, who were not followers, never did accept the fact that Jesus had been raised from the dead. Pretend you are one of those who witnessed the events surrounding *The Resurrection*. Write an entry in your diary describing what you heard and saw and felt.

Dear Diary,

I am so excited I can hardly write today. You'll never believe what happened! I ...

PUTTING IT TOGETHER

Each of the Gospels has an account of Jesus' resurrection. In order to gain the most complete picture of this event, each of the narratives is needed. These stories in Matthew, Mark, Luke, and John tell of personal experiences with the risen Jesus from the perspectives of different witnesses. Use the chart, "The Resurrection of Jesus," to discover the similarities and differences in the records of the accounts of *The Resurrection*.

THE RESURRECTION OF JESUS

Who went to the tomb?

Matthew 28:1–10 _____

_____

Mark 16:1–8 _____

_____

Luke 24:1–12 _____

_____

John 20:1–18 _____

_____

What did they see there?

Matthew 28:1–10 _____

_____

Mark 16:1–8 _____

_____

Luke 24:1–12 _____

_____

John 20:1–18 _____

_____

What were they told to do?

Matthew 28:1–10 _____

_____

Mark 16:1–8 _____

_____

Luke 24:1–12 _____

_____

John 20:1–18 _____

_____

Whom did they tell?

Matthew 28:1–10 _____

_____

Mark 16:1–8 _____

_____

Luke 24:1–12 _____

_____

John 20:1–18 _____

_____

REFLECTION

1. Reflect upon Jesus' question to Mary, "Whom are you looking for?" What do you think Mary was expecting to find? Imagine that Jesus is asking you the same question. How do you respond? What thoughts and feelings do you have?

2. As Christians we are called "Easter people." What does that term mean to you?

Richard Avery and Donald Marsh wrote a hymn titled, "Every Morning is Easter Morning." The text claims that "every day's resurrection day, the past is over and gone!" Think about their proclamation. What does this good news mean to you?

The symbol for *The Spirit* is flames, representing the tongues of fire at Pentecost. (Acts 2:3)

The Spirit

THE STORY CONTINUES

"...Lord, is this the time when you will restore the kingdom to Israel?" He replied, "It is not for you to know the times or periods that the Father has set by his own authority. But you will receive power when the Holy Spirit has come upon you; and you will be my witnesses in Jerusalem, in all Judea and Samaria, and to the ends of the earth." Acts 1:6b-8

Following his resurrection, Jesus is present with his disciples for forty days; then he ascends into heaven. As the disciples watch, angels not only promise that Jesus will return, but also remind them that they have a mission to perform. Jesus' departure is the beginning of ministry for his disciples. Remembering Jesus' command, the disciples remain in Jerusalem and wait for the empowerment of the Holy Spirit.

Fifty days after the resurrection, during the festival of Pentecost, the expectant disciples are filled with the powerful presence of the Holy Spirit. In bold and dynamic ways they preach the good news of Jesus Christ to the assembled festival crowds. Those who listen to the disciples' enthusiastic preaching hear the transforming proclamation that in Jesus the ancient prophecies have been fulfilled. Jesus is the promised Messiah. Even though he was killed, God raised him from the dead, and at this moment God offers forgiveness of sins and a promise of new life to all. The only appropriate response to such good news is to ask, "What shall we do?" Peter urges the crowd to "Repent, and be baptized." Many do repent and are baptized that same day.

The beginning of the Christian church is remembered as the day when the timid became bold, the weak became strong, and the innocent became wise. The proclamation of Jesus Christ as Lord and Savior is transforming. The message must be shared!

PREPARING FOR THE SEARCH

These terms and names will be important as you begin reading about *The Spirit.*

Acts of the Apostles, is a book whose contents span the first decades of the history of the church. It tells the story of God's Holy Spirit guiding the growth of the community of believers from a small group in Jerusalem to a worldwide church extending to Rome, the capital of the empire. It also tells about the career of Paul. Both the Gospel of Luke and The Acts of the Apostles are addressed by Luke to a friend named Theophilus.

Apostle means "one who is sent," "a messenger," or "an ambassador." When the word is used in the Gospels it refers to the twelve disciples who were chosen by Jesus to share the events of his life, learn from him, and be witnesses of his resurrection. When another apostle, Matthias, was selected to replace Judas, they chose one who had been with Jesus from the beginning and had also seen Jesus after his resurrection. Paul also calls himself an apostle because he believed Jesus appeared to him and commissioned him to preach to the Gentiles. By the mid-second century the term is more widely used and no longer refers to an official group in the church.

Barnabas, whose name can mean "son of encouragement," was a member of the Jerusalem Church who welcomed Saul after his conversion and introduced him to the apostles. Along with his cousin Mark, Barnabas accompanied Paul on the first missionary journey to Cyprus, his home. He later separated from Paul over a disagreement involving Mark. However, the split did not end their friendship. Some traditions identify Barnabas as the author of the Letter to the Hebrews.

Hellenists, referred to in Acts 6:1, were probably Greek-speaking Jewish Christians.

Holy Spirit (see Discovery 18)

Matthias, although not one of the Twelve, had been one of Jesus' disciples from the very beginning. Therefore, when the apostles chose a new apostle to fill Judas' place, Matthias had the right qualifications: length of discipleship and a witness to Jesus' resurrection. (Acts 1:21–26)

Pentecost (pen'tuh-kawst), fifty days after Passover, was the closing celebration of the grain harvest. It is also called the Day of the Firstfruits, Feast of Harvest, or Feast of Weeks. The Christian Church looks back to the first Pentecost after Jesus' resurrection, when the Holy Spirit came upon the waiting disciples and empowered them to continue Christ's mission, as the birthday of the church. (Acts 2)

Philip, one of the seven men chosen to be deacons in the early church, went to proclaim the gospel in Samaria after Stephen was killed. His ministry of preaching and healing resulted in many converts. One key episode in the spread of the gospel was his role in God's conversion of the Ethiopian eunuch, who was traveling from Jerusalem to Gaza. Philip settled in Caesarea and was visited twenty years later by Paul on one of his journeys.

Repentance means "to turn back, to feel sorry, to change one's mind." When the English word "repentance" is used in the Bible it is usually a translation of either the Hebrew words *naham,* which means "to feel sorry;" *shub,* which means "to turn back;" or the Greek word *metanoia,* which means both "to turn back" and "to change one's mind." Jesus not only issued a call to repentance but proclaimed God's promise of forgiveness.

Stephen, a key leader in the Jerusalem Church, became the first martyr of the Christian faith when he was arrested, examined by the Jewish Sanhedrin, and stoned to death because of his witness to Jesus as God's Messiah. (The Jews were permitted to stone to death those who were accused of crimes against God, such as blasphemy, as well as some crimes against others, such as adultery.)

THE SEARCH BEGINS

Read these passages to discover more about the empowering of the early church by God's Spirit. The notes that you make will help you retell the story of *The Spirit.* As you read, reflect on these questions:

- *What was the effect of Pentecost on the followers of Jesus?*
- *How did the early church continue Jesus' ministry?*
- *What were the characteristics of the early church?*

Acts 1:1–11, Jesus' Ascension

Acts 1:12–26, Matthias is Chosen

Acts 2:1–47, The Day of Pentecost

Acts 4:1–22, Peter and John before the Council

Acts 4:23–37, The Believers are Empowered

Acts 6:1–7, The Apostles Organize

Acts 6:8–15; 7:51–60, The Story of Stephen

Acts 8:4–25, The Gospel is Preached

THE SEARCH CONTINUES

In these readings I have questions about...

In these readings I discovered...

FOCUSING THE SEARCH

When we study the Bible and seek to know more about its message, it helps to know something about the original languages, especially some of the most important Hebrew and Greek words. "Spirit" is one of those words.

The Hebrew word for Spirit, *ruach,* and the Greek word, *pneuma,* can also be translated as "wind" and "breath." (The words translate into Latin as *spiritus.*)

When translators come across the words *ruach* in the Old Testament and *pneuma* in the New Testament they must decide what English word should be used. In some passages more than one choice is possible. Therefore it is useful to compare several translations. Genesis 1:2 is a good example of ways in which the Hebrew word *ruach* is translated. Footnotes (fn.) often add additional possibilities.

NRSV (mighty) wind; fn. spirit (of God), wind (of God)

RSV Spirit (of God); fn. wind

NJB (divine) wind; fn. This is not the Spirit of God

NEB (mighty) wind

NIV Spirit (of God)

TEV power (of God); fn. spirit (of God), wind (from God), or (an awesome) wind

In the New Testament the word *pneuma* usually is not rendered in so many different ways. In Acts 2:2 all of the above translations use the word "wind," although the adjectives describing it vary. In Acts 2:4 *pneuma* is translated as "Spirit."

Read John 3:1–8 and note the different translations of *pneuma* which appear in verses 6 and 8. How does this information add to your understanding of the text? Jot down your conclusions here.

PUTTING IT TOGETHER

Knowing the various meanings for the Hebrew and Greek words for "Spirit" is helpful. However, our ultimate understanding comes about when we discover the activity of the Spirit. Read the following passages to discover answers to these questions:

- *What are the acts of the Holy Spirit?*
- *What does the Holy Spirit equip others to do?*

Acts 1:2 _____

Acts 1:8 _____

Acts 2:4 _____

Acts 2:17 _____

Acts 4:31 _____

Acts 9:17 _____

Acts 9:31 _____

Acts 11:15–17 _____

Acts 13:2 _____

Acts 16:6 _____

Acts 19:6 _____

Acts 20:22–23 _____

Complete this sentence:
The Holy Spirit ...

REFLECTION

1. Think about the story of Pentecost. What strike you as the most surprising, amazing, and exciting parts of the story?

In what ways have you personally felt and experienced God's Holy Spirit?

2. Consider the following insights into the life of the early church:

"They devoted themselves to the apostles' teaching and fellowship, to the breaking of bread and the prayers." (Acts 2:42)

"Now the whole group of those who believed were of one heart and soul, and no one claimed private ownership of any possessions, but everything they owned was held in common." (Acts 4:32)

Which aspect of the early church's life appeals to you the most? In what ways is your church seeking to live in community like this? What can you contribute to make this happen?

The symbol for *The Mission* is broken prison bars. God miraculously rescued Peter from prison. (Acts 12:7)

The Mission

THE STORY CONTINUES

He asked, "Do you understand what you are reading?" He replied, "How can I, unless someone guides me?" Acts 8:30–31

Good news is impossible to keep secret, especially since the news is life-giving and life-changing for all people. Philip is eager to share the good news of Jesus Christ, and seizes the opportunity with an Ethiopian official who is reading, but not understanding, a text from the scroll of Isaiah. Philip explains that the prophet was speaking about Jesus Christ, who in his suffering became Savior and Lord. In response to the life-giving message, the official believes in Jesus Christ and asks to be baptized. This kind of encounter repeats itself over and over again as the church expands in mission.

The exciting news that Jesus is alive cannot be kept a secret, especially since the power of the Holy Spirit is directing people into opportunities to share the good news of Jesus Christ. Others eagerly respond in belief and trust; the message of love and forgiveness that is preached sets them free. In believing and trusting the message of God's love, they receive an assurance of God's presence and guidance. When they share the good news, others see and embrace that news as good. We do not know what the newly-baptized Ethiopian official does once he leaves Philip, but we do know that the good news of Jesus Christ is impossible to keep secret.

The tremendous growth of the church through the power of the Holy Spirit is chronicled in The Acts of the Apostles. Another possible title for Luke's book is, "The Acts of the Holy Spirit." As the church grows and organizes, numerous questions must be answered, such as, "Does one continue to obey Jewish Law when one becomes a Christian?" The answer to that question from the Jerusalem Council in Acts 15 is decisive for the future of the Church's mission.

PREPARING FOR THE SEARCH

These people and places are included in the readings for *The Mission.*

Ananias (an'uh-ni'uhs), a Christian living in Damascus, was given a vision of God's conversion of Saul, which happened as Saul journeyed to Damascus to persecute the followers of Jesus. In Ananias' vision, God commissioned him to place his hands upon Saul so that his sight would be restored, he would receive the Holy Spirit, and would be baptized. (Acts 9:10–19)

Antioch in Syria, one of two cities called Antioch in the New Testament, was where the followers of Jesus were first called Christians. (Acts 11:26) Paul and Barnabas taught in the church there for more than a year, and were sent from there on the church's first missionary journey. Antioch, at that time a city of 500,000 inhabitants, was a crucial center of the early church and Paul's home base for other missionary journeys. The other Antioch, in Asia Minor (Acts 13:14–52), was visited twice by Paul on his missionary journeys.

Caesarea, a port on the Mediterranean Sea sixty-five miles northwest of Jerusalem, was the home of Philip, Cornelius the Roman centurion, and the seat of the Roman governors of Palestine. Paul, following his arrest in Jerusalem, was tried in Caesarea before Felix, the Roman governor, and spent two years there in prison. Paul sailed to Rome from Caesarea. (Acts 23:33–26:32)

Christian, the name given to a follower of Jesus Christ, was first applied in Antioch, but it was not used widely. It is found only three times in the New Testament. Jesus' followers were first referred to as "Followers of the Way."

Cornelius, a Roman centurion living in Caesarea, responded to a vision from God and was baptized, along with his household, by the apostle Peter. When Cornelius and all those baptized received the gift of the Holy Spirit, an extremely crucial step in the spread of the gospel took place. They were among the first Gentiles who were converted to Christianity. (Acts 10:1–48)

Damascus, the capital city of Syria, had a large Jewish population and many synagogues. The risen Jesus appeared to Saul on the road from Jerusalem to Damascus.

Joppa, a port thirty-five miles west of Jerusalem, was the home of Simon the Tanner. During the apostle Peter's stay with Simon, he dreamed of "clean" and "unclean" animals. This vision prepared Peter to leave Joppa when he was invited by Cornelius to journey north to Caesarea to baptize his Gentile household.

Paul, whom some have called the founder of Christianity, was first the enemy of the Christians. Then he had a powerful conversion experience. The risen Christ appeared to him while he was traveling to Damascus to seek out Followers of the Way for persecution. After this turnaround in his life, he spent time in Damascus with Ananias and other Christians, preaching in the synagogues. A plot against his life was discovered, and his friends let him down over the city wall to escape. As a Roman citizen with easy access to the entire empire, he became a missionary to both Jews and Gentiles. Through travels and letters, he spread the gospel of Jesus Christ and transformed the Christian faith from a Jewish sect to a worldwide church.

Silas, a respected member of the Jerusalem Church, accompanied Paul on the second missionary journey. Paul and Silas shared a church council in Antioch, a prison in Philippi, a riot in Thessalonica, a nighttime escape to Beroea, and a successful preaching mission in Corinth. He may have helped both Peter and Paul write their letters and is called Silvanus in the letters. (Acts 15:22–18:17)

Tarsus, an educational crossroads of the world at the time of the New Testament, was the birthplace of Paul. Upon becoming a Christian, Paul returned home briefly, but then centered his ministry in Antioch upon the invitation of Barnabas.

THE SEARCH BEGINS

These passages will help you understand more about *The Mission* of the early church. Use the notes you take in the retelling of the story. When you have finished your reading, you will have found the answers to these questions:

- *What methods did the disciples use to spread the gospel?*

- *Who were some of the leaders of the early church?*

- *How did the church's vision expand to include non-Jews?*

Matthew 28:16–20, The Great Commission

Acts 8:26–40, Philip and the Ethiopian

Acts 9:1–31, Saul is Converted

Acts 10:1–48, Peter and Cornelius

Acts 11:19–26, Christians in Antioch

Acts 12:1–19, Peter Freed from Prison

24   238

Acts 15:1–35, The Jerusalem Council

THE SEARCH CONTINUES

In these readings I have questions about...

In these readings I discovered...

FOCUSING THE SEARCH

The extensive mission of the church in the first century depended upon the ministries of many individuals. Although Peter and Paul were the most prominent, others took an active role. Choose one of the leaders in the early church listed below and write a short biography of that person, focusing on questions of who, what, when, where, and why. What difference did that person make in sharing the good news of Jesus? Use the information in "Preparing for the Search" and the Bible references noted next to the names for gathering information.

For additional information on the leader you have chosen, use a Bible dictionary such as *Harper's Bible Dictionary,* published by Harper and Row, and the *New Westminster Dictionary of the Bible,* published by Westminster Press. Your church staff may have other suggestions.

Barnabas: Acts 4:36–37; Acts 11:19–30; Acts 13: 1–3; Acts 13:49–14:3; Acts 15: 1–2, 12; Acts 15:36–41; Colossians 4:10.

John Mark (or Mark): Acts 12:12, 25; Acts 13:1–13; Acts 15:36–40; Colossians 4:10.

Philip the Evangelist: Acts 6:1–6; Acts 8:5–13; Acts 8:26–39; Acts 21:8–9.

Silas: Acts 15:22–41; Acts 16:16–40; Acts 17: 1–15; Acts 18:5.

PUTTING IT TOGETHER

From a dramatic beginning in Jerusalem, the church expanded rapidly throughout the Roman Empire. Whenever we read the New Testament, and especially the book of Acts, it is helpful to use a timeline as a frame of reference. While it is impossible to date many of the events and the writing of the books of the New Testament with precision, the "New Testament Timeline" on page 242 is based on careful estimates. Use it to locate these events and answer the questions that follow.

- *Pentecost in Jerusalem*

- *Paul's Conversion on the road to Damascus*

- *Barnabas joins Paul on the First Missionary Journey*

- *The Jerusalem Council*

- *Silas, Timothy, and Luke join Paul for the Second Missionary Journey*

- *Paul's Third Missionary Journey*

- *Paul's Journey to Rome*

- *Destruction of Jerusalem by Titus/Romans*

1. Approximately how many years passed between Jesus' resurrection and Paul's arrival in Rome? What has happened in that span of time in your own life?

2. How many years separate Jesus' life, death, and resurrection from the writing of the first Gospel? What does that suggest about the ways the stories about Jesus were shared before being written?

3. What does the fact that some of the letters were written before the Gospels suggest to you?

REFLECTION

1. Reflect upon the dramatic story of Paul's conversion to faith in Jesus Christ. What do you feel is the most important aspect of his conversion? In what ways has your own conversion been similar to or different from Paul's?

2. Think about the Ethiopian official who read the Scripture but did not understand. How important is it to have someone interpret the Bible to others? What is most helpful to you when you are seeking to understand the Bible? In what ways do you now see yourself called to help someone else understand the Bible?

New Testament Timeline

B.C.

63 Pompey/Romans
Conquer Palestine

50

37 Herod the Great,
King of the Jews

c.30 Augustus,
Roman Emperor

10

c.6-4 Birth of Jesus

A.D.

10

20

Ministry of Jesus

30   Death and Resurrection of Jesus c.30-33
      Pentecost c.30-33

      Paul's Conversion c.33-37

40

Paul's First Missionary Journey c.46-48

The Jerusalem Council c.49

50   Paul's Second Missionary Journey c.49-52

50-52 1,2 Thessalonians

53-54 Galatians   Paul's Third Missionary Journey c.52-56

54-56 1,2 Corinthians

56-58 Romans   Paul's Journey to Rome c.58-60

54-62 Colossians, Phillipians   60

                     Death of Paul c.64

68-70 Gospel of Mark

70   Destruction of Jerusalem 70

80

85-100 Gospel of Luke/Acts

85-100 Gospel of Matthew   90

90-100 Gospel of John

100

The symbol for *The Journeys* is a ship. The gospel travels throughout the Mediterranean. (Acts 20:13–16)

DISCOVERY 25

The Journeys

THE STORY CONTINUES

He asked, "Who are you, Lord?" Acts 9:5

Saul's journey to Damascus to persecute the followers of Jesus is dramatically interrupted when a blinding light throws him to the ground. His question, asked in fear and trembling, receives an answer that dramatically transforms his life, "I am Jesus, whom you are persecuting... get up and enter the city, and you will be told what you are to do." Saul, whose Roman name was Paul, begins a journey that will take him throughout the world to recruit followers of Jesus. He is one who knows what it means to be transformed by God. First blinded, then restored to sight, he is led into wonderful adventures, dangerous journeys, and exciting opportunities to preach the good news.

Paul travels to many of the major cities of the Roman Empire, taking with him the dynamic message of new life in Jesus Christ. He visits such cities as Antioch, Corinth, Ephesus, Thessalonica, and Philippi, and regions like Galatia. He wins converts, forms churches, corresponds with those churches, and when possible revisits them. Out of his own experiences of courage, defeat, imprisonment, hospitality, danger and generosity, he interprets and communicates, especially by letter, the fullness of life in Jesus Christ. When questioned, attacked, and persecuted by those opposing the gospel, he stands firm in his defense, responding that God in Jesus Christ is working through him.

From a small beginning, the gospel of Jesus Christ travels throughout the world. Jesus' ministry came to completion in Jerusalem, center of Israel's faith and hope. From there the apostles spread the proclamation of **good news** throughout the world. Paul's ministry comes to completion in Rome, the center of the most extensive empire the world has known. From Rome, the good news will continue to be preached around the world.

PREPARING FOR THE SEARCH

The names of these people and places are important in the story of *The Journeys*.

Athens, one of the great cities of the ancient world, was still a center for learning when the apostle Paul visited on his second missionary journey around 50 A.D. Paul caught the attention of the philosophers and engaged them in discussion by noticing an altar that was dedicated "To an Unknown God." Paul proclaimed the gospel of Jesus Christ, God who is known. (Acts 17:15–34)

Damaris (dam'uh-ris), a woman, and **Dionysius** (di-uh-nee'suhs), a member of the Areopagite council in Athens, were among Paul's few converts in that city. (Acts 17:34)

Barnabas. See Discovery 23.

Eutychus (yoo' tuh-kuhs) was a youth whose Greek name means "fortunate." Late at night Paul was preaching in an upstairs room in the city of Troas when Eutychus went to sleep, fell out of the window, and was presumed dead on the street three stories below. Paul went down, embraced him, and assured those present that Eutychus was alive. (Acts 20:7–12)

Lydia, a seller of purple-dyed fabric, became a Christian when Paul preached in Philippi. She was Paul's first convert to Christianity in Macedonia and Europe. As a leader of the Philippian Church, she housed Paul and Silas during their stay. (Acts 16:14–15,40)

Macedonia, a Roman province in northern Greece, included the cities of Thessalonica, Philippi, and Beroea. After Paul responded to the vision of a Macedonian man asking for help, the region became the beachhead for the spread of the gospel in Europe. The Macedonians contributed generously to the needs of the members in the Jerusalem Church. (Acts 16:8–17:15)

Philippi (fil' uh-pi), a Macedonian city eight miles inland from the Aegean Sea, was the home of a large Roman colony. Paul visited Philippi on his second missionary journey in response to a vision, and the mission to Europe began. Converts to the Christian faith included Lydia, the possessed slave girl, and, during Paul's imprisonment, his jailer. (Acts 16:11–40)

Rome, capital of the immense Roman Empire, was the center of the ancient world by the time of the birth of Jesus and the spread of the Christian faith. All roads led to Rome. When Paul visited Rome late in his ministry, a Christian church was active there, perhaps due to visitors from Rome who were in Jerusalem on Pentecost. Paul was under guard for two years in Rome.

Peter was also in Rome; and, according to tradition, Peter and Paul were both martyred during Emperor Nero's persecution of the Christians.

Timothy, a young Christian from Lystra, became Paul's faithful companion and co-worker on the second missionary journey. On Paul's first missionary journey to Lystra, Timothy's mother, Eunice, and grandmother, Lois, had been converted to faith in Jesus Christ. Paul chose Timothy to accompany him to Thessalonica, Corinth, and Ephesus. Timothy stayed in Ephesus and became the leader of the church. Two letters in the New Testament bear his name. They are full of encouragement and advice for the young pastor as he faithfully leads the church in Ephesus.

Troas, a port near ancient Troy (northwest Turkey), was where Paul had the vision which began the Christian mission to Macedonia and Europe. It was in Troas that Eutychus fell asleep during one of Paul's long sermons.

THE SEARCH BEGINS

The story of Paul's journeys to spread the gospel is exciting. As he and his companions told the good news about Jesus in town after town and country after country, the church increased dramatically. Although the passages listed give you an overview of this period, the only way to get the full picture is to read Acts 13 through 28. Take notes that will help you retell the story of *The Journeys*. Consider these questions as you read:

- *In what ways were Paul's journeys crucial to the growth of the church?*

- *How would you describe the response to the proclamation of the good news of Jesus Christ?*

- *What was it that convinced those who heard Paul's preaching to become believers?*

Acts 13:1–3, 42–52; 14:21–28, Paul's First Journey

Acts 15:36–16:10, Paul's Second Journey

Acts 16:11–40, Prison in Philippi

Acts 17:16–34, Paul in Athens

Acts 20:1–38, Paul's Third Journey

Acts 21:17, 27–36, Paul in Jerusalem

Acts 28:16–31, Paul in Rome

THE SEARCH CONTINUES

In these readings I have questions about...

In these readings I discovered...

FOCUSING THE SEARCH

Paul's letters are not just ancient documents. They continue to live as vibrant expressions of the good news of Jesus Christ. Paul either initiated a dialogue with the churches in his letters or responded to letters and visitors he received. Often, his letters resulted in additional letters being exchanged. In expressing the good news of Jesus Christ, Paul was in dialogue with his partners in the gospel. The following exercise will help you appreciate that when letters from Paul were received they invited a response.

Imagine you are one of the Christians in Rome and have just heard Paul's letter to your church read in worship. You are especially moved by the section that reads:

For I am convinced that neither death, nor life, nor angels, nor rulers, nor things present, nor things to come, nor powers, nor height, nor depth, nor anything else in all creation, will be able to separate us from the love of God in Christ Jesus our Lord. (Romans 8:38–39)

Respond to his message of God's grace in Jesus Christ by telling Paul what his letter has meant to you. Write your letter here.

From _____ to Paul, my friend in the faith:

Now picture yourself in worship as these moving words from Paul's letter to the church in Philippi are read:

Rejoice in the Lord always; again I will say, Rejoice. Let your gentleness be known to everyone. The Lord is near. Do not worry about anything, but in everything by prayer and supplication with thanksgiving let your requests be made known to God. And the peace of God, which surpasses all understanding, will guard your hearts and your minds in Christ Jesus. (Philippians 4:4–7)

Respond to this encouraging message of God's care by writing your prayer, putting your thanksgivings and requests in words. You may be asked to share this prayer at the close of the session.

Loving God, ...

PUTTING IT TOGETHER

Paul's four journeys are difficult to keep clear in our minds. It is useful, however, to be aware of the range of Paul's travels when reading about them in The Acts of the Apostles. Using four different colored pencils, trace the following journeys on the map on page 251.

Paul's First Missionary Journey: Antioch, Cyprus, Perga, Pisidian Antioch, Iconium, Lystra, Derbe.

Paul's Second Missionary Journey: Jerusalem, Caesarea, Antioch, Tarsus, Derbe, Lystra, Iconium, Pisidian Antioch, Troas, Philippi, Thessalonica, Beroea, Athens, Corinth, Ephesus, Caesarea.

Paul's Third Missionary Journey: Antioch, Derbe, Lystra, Iconium, Pisidian Antioch, Ephesus, Troas, Philippi, Thessalonica, Corinth, Miletus, Rhodes, Tyre, Caesarea, Jerusalem.

Paul's Journey to Rome: Caesarea, Sidon, Crete, Malta, Syracuse, Rome.

REFLECTION

1. Reflect upon the words of Jesus quoted by Paul in Acts 20:35:

It is more blessed to give than to receive.

These words of Jesus do not appear anywhere else in the Bible. What insights come from reading these additional words of his? At what time in his ministry do you think he may have said them? What do they mean to you?

2. Read these words from Paul's autobiographical sketch in 2 Corinthians:

Three times I was beaten with rods. Once I received a stoning. Three times I was shipwrecked; for a night and a day I was adrift at sea; on frequent journeys, in danger from rivers, danger from bandits, danger from my own people, danger from Gentiles, danger in the city, danger in the wilderness, danger at sea, danger from false brothers and sisters; in toil and hardship, through many a sleepless night, hungry and thirsty, often without food, cold and naked. And besides other things, I am under daily pressure because of my anxiety for all the churches. (2 Corinthians 11:25–28)

What insights do Paul's words give concerning his missionary journeys? What are some dangers the church faces today in the proclamation of the gospel of Christ? What dangers do you face in your journey?

The Journeys of Paul

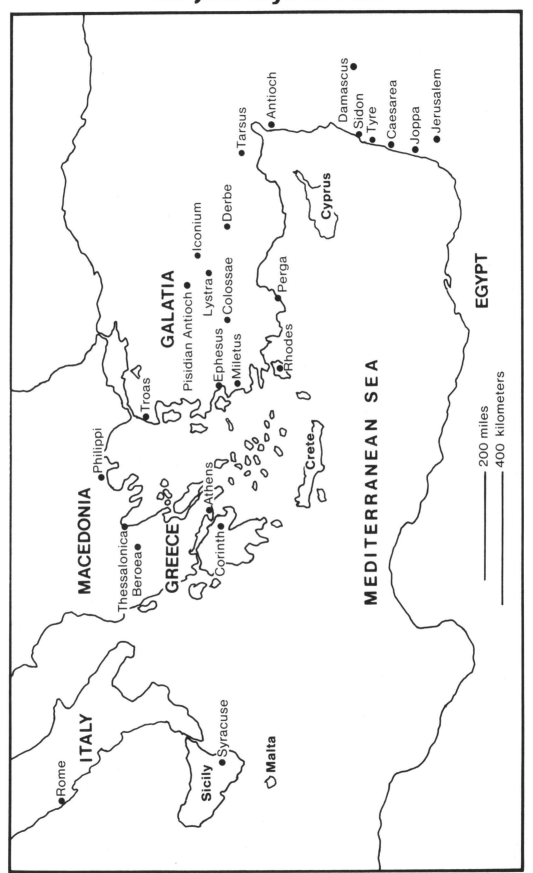

The symbol for *The Proclamation* is the cross of Jesus, representing God's reconciliation. (Colossians 1:20)

The Proclamation

THE STORY CONTINUES

The only thing I want to learn from you is this: Did you receive the Spirit by doing the works of the law or by believing what you heard? Galatians 3:2

Peter's sermon on the day of Pentecost contains the central proclamation (*kerygma*) of the earliest Christian preaching: "...God has made him both Lord and Messiah, this Jesus whom you crucified." (Acts 2:36b) In the resurrection of Jesus and in the powerful indwelling of the Holy Spirit on Pentecost something new and wonderful takes place. "Jesus is Lord," and "Jesus is Messiah," (or Christ), are statements of belief used to communicate God's mighty acts in the life, death, and resurrection of Jesus.

Paul is the one who expands upon the implications of the proclamation "Jesus is Lord." He writes to respond to many of the churches' questions and concerns, especially questions relating to the practice of the Jewish law and how the Christian deals with the faith of Israel. In addressing these concerns, Paul elaborates upon what "Jesus is Lord" means. Writing to the church in Galatia, he takes them to task for their willingness to believe they must rely on keeping the Law to win God's favor. Writing to the church in Colossae, he warns them not to accept beliefs contrary to faith in Jesus Christ.

Many implications of the Christian proclamation are worked out in response to raging controversies. Extended theological arguments are expressed in the letters that circulate among the churches. Words such as sanctification, justification, and redemption are used to explain the fullness of the good news of Jesus Christ. Even so, it is difficult to improve upon the earliest proclamation, "Jesus is Lord."

PREPARING FOR THE SEARCH

The definitions below provide background information for your study of *The Proclamation.*

Colossians. Paul sent his friend Epaphras to preach in Colossae, but he himself never visited there. This letter was written to respond to false teachings that had appeared in the church, and to proclaim the absolute supremacy of Jesus Christ.

1 and 2 Corinthians. These are two of perhaps four or five letters Paul wrote to a church he founded in 50–51 A.D. Written between 54–56 A.D., they focus on problems that the church was facing: disunity, disputes between members, and immoral behavior. Paul responds to their problems, explaining what it means to follow Christ.

Epaphras (ep'uh-fras), a close associate of Paul's, may have been the founder of the church in Colossae. He visited Rome during Paul's imprisonment to tell him about the needs of the Colossian Church.

Faith, a word related to "truth" and "trust," is best defined in Hebrews 11:1, "Now faith is the assurance of things hoped for, the conviction of things not seen." Faith, in the earliest proclamation of the gospel, is possible because of the death and resurrection of Jesus Christ.

Galatians. This letter was written to the churches in Galatia, a region in central Asia Minor. Paul wrote it to correct an error in teaching that stressed that a right relationship with God could only be won through obedience to the Law. He holds that in Jesus' death, the Law has been fulfilled, and Christians (both Jew and Gentile) are no longer under the Law's demands.

Grace, a word that comes from the Greek word *charis* (and thus "charismatic"), refers to the unmerited free gift of redemption in Jesus Christ. Grace is God's gift, received, not earned, in which sin is forgiven and faith strengthened.

James, the brother of Jesus, became the leader of the Jerusalem Church, a crucial position for the spread of the Christian faith. As a respected Jewish Christian, he was influential in admitting and welcoming Gentiles into the Christian Church. Jesus' resurrection appearance to James, as it is recorded, is perhaps an indication of James' Easter conversion to faith in Jesus as the Son of God. (1 Corinthians 15:7)

Justified comes from the Greek word for acquittal and means that God has acted in the death and resurrection of Jesus Christ to acquit all who believe, to set them free from sin. To be justified is to have a right relationship with God restored because of faith in Jesus Christ.

Kerygma, a Greek word meaning "proclamation," refers to the content rather than the manner of the Christian proclamation: the *kerygma* is the life, death, and resurrection of Jesus Christ.

Law, when used in the Bible, refers specifically to the Law given by God to Moses on Mount Sinai, and generally to the TORAH, the first five books of the Bible, which provide further law codes and commentaries on the law of Moses.

Reconciliation means putting together that which has been separated. It is an accurate description of God's mighty acts. The biblical story tells of the break between God and humanity soon after creation. The story continues with God's relentless work to reconcile, to put together, to heal creation. Although individuals are encouraged to be reconciled to one another, the word is used most often in the New Testament to refer to God's activity in bringing about reconciliation with humanity.

Redemption, a word which literally means "to buy back," is used in the New Testament to refer to being freed from bondage to sin and death by Christ's death and resurrection.

Righteousness, a key word and concept throughout the Bible, means "being in the right" and "being vindicated." God brings about righteousness, and in the death and resurrection of Jesus, God has made us righteous.

Romans. The letter to the Romans is the longest and most carefully written of all Paul's letters. It was probably composed between 55–58 A.D., toward the end of his career. Although Paul had not been to Rome, the letter clearly indicates that he hopes to visit that church. In writing extensively on theological issues, Paul explains and defends the gospel, preparing the people in Rome for his visit.

Salvation, which has many shades of meaning in the Bible, refers to God's act of rescue from sin and death and the sense of peace and reconciliation with God which comes with the acceptance of God's gift. God's salvation is past, present, and future.

Sanctification is the process of being made or becoming holy. Through Jesus Christians are said to be sanctified or set apart for God's purposes. On the other hand, Christians are always striving to become sanctified in the sense of becoming more completely devoted to doing God's will.

THE SEARCH BEGINS

The passages listed below contain information about some of the issues Paul thought were important parts of *The Proclamation*. In the notes you take, record two to five main points for each passage. These questions can help guide your reading:

- *What did Paul believe was the heart of the Christian message?*

- *What was the content of the earliest Christian preaching?*

- *What are the results of faith in Jesus Christ?*

Romans 1:16–17, The Gospel's Power

Romans 5:1–11, Saved by Christ

1 Corinthians 1:18–31, The "Foolish" Message

1 Corinthians 15:1–11, The Gospel

2 Corinthians 4:1–15, Spiritual Treasure

Galatians 1:1–10, One Gospel

Galatians 3:1–14, Faith, not Law

Galatians 3:19–4:7, Oneness in Christ

Colossians 1:1–14, A Prayer for Understanding

Colossians 1:15–23, Christ, the Likeness of God

THE SEARCH CONTINUES

In these readings I have questions about...

In these readings I discovered...

FOCUSING THE SEARCH

Paul's letters, originally written in Greek, have been translated into most of the world's languages. The task of a translator is not to provide a word for word or even a phrase for phrase translation from Greek to English. As you can see from the word for word translation of Romans 1:16–17 below, that type of a rendition is not very helpful.

ROMANS 1:16,17
(A literal rendering)

16) For I am not ashamed-of the good-news, for it is God's power into[1] deliverance/salvation to everyone who is (keeps on) believing/trusting, to Jews first and also to Greek;

17) for God's righteousness/uprightness/justice is being uncovered/revealed out of faith/faithfulness into[1] faith/ faithfulness, as it has-been-written, And the upright/just/righteous [man][2] out of faith/faithfulness will live.

[1]The preposition is literally "into," but it may be translated "unto,"/"with a purpose of."

[2]The article and adjective (-substantive/noun) are in masculine gender. It would not do, of course, to use neuter, and there is no common gender. It is therefore legitimate to translate "person."

Instead, translators try to communicate the author's message in a "dynamic cultural equivalent." Romans 1:16–17 is recorded below as it is printed in three different English translations: *The Revised Standard Version,* published in 1952, *Today's English Version,* first published in 1966, and the *New Revised Standard Version,* published in 1990. Read these translations and then write out the two verses from another translation such as the *New Jerusalem Bible, New English Bible,* or the *New International Version.*

> For I am not ashamed of the gospel; it is the power of God for salvation to every one who has faith, to the Jew first and also to the Greek. For in it the righteousness of God is revealed through faith for faith; as it is written, "He who through faith is righteous shall live." *RSV*

> For I am not ashamed of the gospel; it is the power of God for salvation to everyone who has faith, to the Jew first and also to the Greek. For in it the righteousness of God is revealed through faith for faith; as it is written, "The one who is righteous will live by faith." *NRSV*

> I have complete confidence in the gospel; it is God's power to save all who believe, first the Jews and also the Gentiles. For the gospel reveals how God puts people right with himself; it is through faith from beginning to end. As the scripture says, "The person who is put right with God through faith shall live." *TEV*

Compare the four. Which translation do you think best communicates the message? Why?

PUTTING IT TOGETHER

Knowledge of the historical situation that prompted the writing of Paul's letters helps with their interpretation. In this session you looked at portions of letters to churches at Rome, Corinth, Galatia, and Colossae. Select one of these and locate further information about the situation facing that church, using one of the following resources that are available in your church library:

> a. Study Bible (i.e., *The New Oxford Annotated BIble, Revised Standard Version, Oxford Study Edition of the New English Bible,* etc.).
>
> b. Bible dictionary (i.e., the *New Westminster Bible Dictionary, Harper's Bible Dictionary,* etc.).
>
> c. Bible handbook (i.e., *Abingdon Bible Handbook* or *Illustrated Bible Handbook*).
>
> d. Bible commentary (on Romans, Corinthians, Galatians, or Colossians).

You may be asked to share your information with the group.

REFLECTION

1. Reflect upon the lyrics of the hymn "Amazing Grace." These words could be Paul's: "I once was blind but now I see."

In what way have you been given sight? In what areas in your life do you seek further light? How do you see things differently because of your faith and trust in God?

2. Paul wrote to the Corinthians about the "foolishness" of the gospel. What do you think he meant by this as he wrote to them? What do Paul's words say to you?

The symbol for *The Church* is a communion cup, representing our unity in Christ. (1 Corinthians 11:25–26)

DISCOVERY 27

The Church

THE STORY CONTINUES

Do you not know that you are God's temple and that God's Spirit dwells in you? 1 Corinthians 3:16

Paul travels throughout the Roman Empire to preach, teach, and establish new churches. He also writes letters to proclaim the gospel of Christ and to address problems that are affecting the growth and mission of the Church. For instance, divisions apparently exist within the church in Corinth; people observe the Lord's Supper with disregard for one another's needs. In his letter to the Corinthians, Paul angrily questions their understanding of the sacred meal. It is another opportunity for Paul to instruct and demonstrate his continuing care for one of the churches he founded.

In many of his letters Paul helps solve problems in the churches: jealousy among the leadership, divisiveness within the church, promises made and forgotten, misunderstandings about the gospel, and competing claims about discipleship. Paul does not set out to write "Scripture," but God so inspires his writing, and his letters so illuminate the good news of Jesus Christ, that they are collected and treasured. Paul reminds those involved in the leadership struggles in the churches of their call to be servants, following the example of Christ's servanthood. To those who are part of the divisive factions, he emphasizes unity in Christ: one body, one faith, one Spirit, one hope, one Lord. He seeks offerings to relieve the financial problems of the Jerusalem church. Other leaders, addressing similar concerns, also write letters to the churches.

In attending to the practical concerns of first century Christians, Paul and other writers, named and unnamed, lay down the pattern for the church's life to be followed for centuries, to the present day.

PREPARING FOR THE SEARCH

Read about these words that have special meaning in *The Church*.

Apollos, an educated Alexandrian Jew who met Aquila and Priscilla in Ephesus, became very active in the church in Corinth. His involvement caused some people to form an "Apollos group." Apparently there was no conflict between Paul and Apollos, because Paul understood that there are different talents and functions in the church. (Acts 18:24–28; 19:1)

Ephesians, written by Paul or one of Paul's disciples, was sent to the churches in the area of Ephesus to explain God's divine plan as it relates to Christ, the church, and the Christian life.

Gifts (of the Holy Spirit) are enumerated in many of Paul's letters, including 1 Corinthians 12:4–11, 28–30. These attributes are bestowed by God and are to be used to build up the Kingdom.

Lord's Supper is a name given by Paul to the sacred meal commemorating Jesus' final meal with his disciples before his death. Our understanding of the Lord's Supper, and much of our contemporary observance, comes from Paul's comments in 1 Corinthians 11:17–34.

1 Peter. This letter, which seems to be more of a sermon than an epistle, may have originally been used to provide instruction about baptism. Addressed to "the exiles of the Dispersion...," it encourages members of the Christian community to hold firmly to their faith, even in times of persecution. If the apostle Peter is not the actual author of this letter, he probably inspired it.

1 and 2 Thessalonians. These two letters, written by Paul to the church at Thessalonica, talk of hope in Christ and respond to questions about Christ's return. The first letter, written about 50 A.D., is perhaps the oldest of the preserved letters of Paul.

THE SEARCH BEGINS

Letters to the churches provide clues about the ways this young community functioned. As you read the passages listed below, you will discover some of the concerns and some of the joys that are reflected in these writings to *The Church*. In notes that you make for each passage, list three to five of the major points being made. These questions can guide your reading:

- *What problems were being faced by the churches?*
- *What "gifts" have been bestowed by God's Spirit?*
- *How are Christians to act?*

1 Corinthians 3:1–23, Conflict and Cooperation

1 Corinthians 11:17–34, The Lord's Supper

1 Corinthians 12:1–31, Gifts for the Body of Christ

1 Corinthians 13:1–13, The Greatest Gift

1 Corinthians 16:1–4; 2 Corinthians 9:1–15, The Collection
for Christians in Jerusalem

Ephesians 2:11–22, United in Christ

Ephesians 4:1–16, One Lord, One Spirit

1 Thessalonians 5:12–28, Life in Community

1 Peter 2:1–10, A Spiritual Household

THE SEARCH CONTINUES

In these readings I have questions about...

In these readings I discovered...

FOCUSING THE SEARCH

"Remember" is one of the most important words in the Christian faith. Jesus, when he celebrated the meal in the Upper Room with his disciples, said to them, "Do this in remembrance of me." (Luke 22:19) From its beginning, the church has centered its worship around the Lord's Supper and has gathered to remember Jesus.

The four Gospels tell the story of Jesus' meal with his disciples in the Upper Room. 1 Corinthians offers the earliest description of the celebration of the Lord's Supper.

To find out more about the Lord's Supper review the passages that are indicated. Use the information you discover to answer the questions listed below.

THE LAST SUPPER OF THE LORD

Matthew 26:17–30; Mark 14:12–26; Luke 22:1–23; John 13:1–38

a. Who was present?

b. When and where was the meal eaten?

c. What happened during the meal?

d. What reason is given for its celebration?

THE EARLY CHURCH CELEBRATES THE LORD'S SUPPER

1 Corinthians 11:17–34

a. Who was present?

b. When and where was the meal eaten?

c. What happened during the meal?

d. Why was it celebrated by the church?

THE LORD'S SUPPER TODAY

a. Which elements noted above are reflected in the way your congregation celebrates this sacrament of the church?

b. What insights did you gain about the celebration of the Lord's Supper?

c. What does it mean to you to participate in this sacrament?

PUTTING IT TOGETHER

Paul was a superb teacher. Like Jesus, he drew upon everything that he saw around him to communicate the good news. In order to transform the mind and heart of the reader or the listener, Paul and other New Testament writers often used everyday images to communicate the message of the gospel.

Using your imagination, draw on another sheet of paper one of the images of the church that is depicted in these passages.

1 Corinthians 3:6–7. Plant and Water

1 Corinthians 3:9–17. A Company of Builders

1 Corinthians 12:12–31. One Body with Many Parts

Ephesians 2:20–22. The Cornerstone

1 Peter 2:4–10. A Spiritual Temple

What contemporary images communicate a truth about the church of Jesus Christ? From among the images you see around you, select one that would have been unknown by Paul. Write a few sentences that explain how the image you selected embodies some truth about the church.

The church is like...

REFLECTION

1. Meditate on what Paul discovered about love:

Love is patient. Love is kind...It bears all things, believes all things, hopes all things, endures all things. (1 Corinthians 13:4, 7)

How do you think Paul came to know this? What do Paul's words say to you? What have you discovered about love?

2. Reflect upon Paul's constant emphasis on the Christian community's "oneness in Christ." What does this image say to you about current relations within the worldwide church? within the local church? What need in your life do these words address? What does oneness in Christ mean to you?

The symbol for *The New Life* is a vine and heart, depicting Jesus' words, "I am the vine, you are the branches...love one another as I have loved you." (John 15:5a, 12)

DISCOVERY 28

The New Life

THE STORY CONTINUES

Should we continue in sin in order that grace may abound? By no means! How can we who died to sin go on living in it? Romans 6:1b-2

Unity in Jesus Christ is a major concern for the early church because everyone who is now a part of the church is a convert from another religion. The first followers of Jesus are Jews. In fact, the good news of Jesus Christ is first proclaimed in the Temple and the synagogues. As the gospel spreads throughout the world, converts from other religions, philosophies, and practices accept Jesus Christ as Lord and Savior and are baptized into the church. Everyone, Jew and Gentile alike, is new to the Christian way of believing and acting.

Paul's question concerning faith and action directly addresses a question the early Christians have about the new life they are called to live. In addition to confessing faith in Jesus Christ, new "Christians" are called to embrace a way of living that expresses that faith. So they ask, "Do we continue to practice the Jewish law? If we do not follow the Law, what does guide our actions? Doesn't Christ's imminent return make our concerns inconsequential anyway?"

Paul and other leaders elaborate on the new life in Christ in every letter they write to the churches. In his letter to the church in Rome Paul calls for a complete transformation in thinking and acting. In the one to the church in Galatia he describes the "fruits of the Spirit" that characterize the new life. The letter to the church in Colossae compares the new life with the garments one wears. The letters to individuals like Timothy spell out the demands and rewards of the new life. In every instance, the new life is contrasted with the old life in order to make clear the ways God transforms lives. The letters written by Paul and other leaders are passed from church to church, read over and over, and treasured as God's truth. Each new convert to faith in Jesus Christ is helped by being told clearly what it means to follow Christ – faith, hope, and love, a new way of living.

PREPARING FOR THE SEARCH

Refer back to this information as you read the passages that tell the story of *The New Life.*

James. Written primarily for Jewish Christians, the letter responds to problems of the church at large. It may have been used as a book to instruct new Christians. The writer's attitude towards the importance of works ("For just as the body without the spirit is dead, so faith without works is also dead." 2:26) contrasts with Paul's.

1 John was written to counteract false teachings about Jesus that were undermining the faithful. The author writes to reassure them that the message of the gospel can be trusted. He encourages them to love God and one another.

2 Timothy. Like 1 Timothy and Titus, 2 Timothy contains practical information about the difficult role of the pastor. It is also an earnest plea from a veteran missionary to a younger colleague, urging him to hold fast to the gospel, be patient, and endure.

THE SEARCH BEGINS

The passages below describe *The New Life* of those who have faith in Jesus Christ. As you read, take notes that list the attributes of those following this new life and consider these questions:

- *What does it mean to be a Christian?*
- *How do the writers understand the new life in Jesus Christ?*
- *What words of wisdom are imparted?*

Romans 12:1–21, Transformed Lives

Galatians 5:16–6:10, The Fruits of the Spirit

Ephesians 4:17–5:2, The New Life

Colossians 3:1–17, The New Life

2 Timothy 2:1–26, A Loyal Soldier

James 2:14–26, Faith and Actions

1 Peter 1:3–9, 13–22, A Living Hope

1 John 4:7–21, God is Love

THE SEARCH CONTINUES

In these readings I have questions about...

In these readings I discovered...

FOCUSING THE SEARCH

For the early converts, professing faith in Jesus Christ and being baptized into the community of believers meant promising to live in a new way. In order to underscore this new way of living, Paul made liberal use of contrasts: old and new, darkness and light, law and grace, and so on. One way to discover the force of these contrasts is to devise other comparisons using words that are the opposite of Paul's. For instance, consider the words, "Let love be genuine; hate what is evil." The contrasting thought is, "Let love be fake; love what is evil."

Below rewrite at least five verses of Romans 12:9–18 so that they say the opposite of Paul's meaning.

How does this exercise help you feel the impact of Paul's admonition to live a new life?

PUTTING IT TOGETHER

One of the major contrasts the New Testament makes is the contrast between the old life in sin and the new life in Christ. Use the chart, "The New Life in Christ," to discover how this contrast is portrayed in the letters to the Galatians and the Colossians.

THE NEW LIFE IN CHRIST

Two letters to young churches say clearly what it means to live as a Christian. Read the following sections of the letters to the churches at Galatia and Colossae, and fill in the blanks. You will see the contrasts between the "old" life in sin and the "new" life in Christ.

Galatians 5:19–23

"Now the works of the flesh are obvious...   By contrast, the fruit of the Spirit is:

fornication   _____

impurity   _____

licentiousness   _____

idolatry   _____

sorcery   _____

enmities   _____

strife   _____

jealousy   _____

anger   _____

quarrels   _____

dissensions   _____

factions   _____

envy   _____

drunkenness   _____

carousing, etc.   _____

Colossians 3:5–17

"Put to death, therefore, whatever in you is earthly:	As God's chosen ones, holy and beloved, clothe yourselves with:
fornication	_____
impurity	_____
passion	_____
evil desire	_____
greed	_____
anger	_____
wrath	_____
malice	_____
slander	_____
abusive language	_____

REFLECTION

1. Reflect upon these words of Paul to the Romans: "Do not be conformed to this world, but be transformed by the renewing of your minds, so that you may discern what is the will of God–what is good and acceptable and perfect." (Romans 12:2)

What do you think prompted Paul to write these words? In what ways will a new mind result in a new life? What transformation and renewal do you hope for in your own life?

2. The passages you have read describe the attributes of a Christian. Imagine that in your community being a Christian is a crime punishable by imprisonment. You have been arrested. What evidence can be presented to convict you? In other words, how do others know that you are practicing *The New Life* in Christ?

The symbol for *The Hope* is Alpha and Omega, the A and Z of the Greek alphabet, representing the beginning and the end. (Revelation 21:6)

The Hope

THE STORY CONTINUES

What then are we to say about these things? If God is for us, who is against us? Romans 8:31

Paul's words of hope to the church in Rome address questions about the future with a stirring affirmation of faith. Uncertainty, caused by the threat of persecution, fills the early church with concern. What is going to happen to us? Paul knows full well that there is only one answer to the question. The assurance that nothing will separate them from God encourages hope within those who feel powerful forces working against them.

Jesus, in his life, death, and resurrection, expresses ultimate confidence in God's wonderful future. Jesus preaches, teaches, and lives a message of hope in that future, yet the exact details and timetable remain a mystery.

The exciting news of the eyewitnesses to Jesus' resurrection spreads to those who have not seen, yet believe. As years pass, the message of forgiveness, new life, and hope is preached to those eager to receive the good news of God's salvation. Some Christians expect an immediate cataclysm, God's final act of bringing in the Kingdom. They see and interpret all that is happening around them as necessary signs for the coming of the Kingdom. Others, over a period of years, reflect on Jesus' words and reinterpret their understanding of God's plan for the future. All seem to ask: When will God's Kingdom come? How will it happen? Will I still be alive? Why is God taking so long? In the face of continuing misunderstanding, persecution, and death from the enemies of the good news of Jesus Christ, a question eventually becomes the answer: "If God is for us, who is against us?"

PREPARING FOR THE SEARCH

Knowledge of the words below can assist you in your discovery of *The Hope.*
Also, review the material in Discovery 15, *The Vision.*

Apocalyptic Literature. Revelation, the last book of the New Testament,
takes its name from the Latin word *revelatio,* which means "uncovering,"
"unveiling," "making visible something hidden." The Latin is a translation
of the Greek word *apokalypsis,* which in English is "apocalypse." The book
was written to encourage Christians who were facing severe persecution. It is
an example of a special form of literature that was popular in Judaism from
about 300 B.C. to 100 A.D. Although the book of Revelation is the only vol-
ume in the New Testament that is thoroughly apocalyptic, this type of literature is sprinkled through many other books, such as Matthew, Mark, 2
Thessalonians, Jude, and 2 Peter. The characteristics of apocalyptic include:
supernatural visions, angelic interpreters, widespread use of symbolism, the
division of history into time periods, and the expectation of the nearness of
the end of the age. Written in times of great peril, apocalyptic literature
looks forward to God's intervention in the world's affairs to bring about a
New Age. Some of the hope that is expressed in this Discovery comes from
passages that are written in the traditional apocalyptic form. Examples of
this type of literature in "The Search Begins" are: Matthew 25:31–46, Mark
13:1–37, and the three readings from Revelation.

Glory, a word indicating God's holy presence, is a translation of the Hebrew
word *kabod* which means "honor" and "splendor." In the life of Israel, the glory
of God was manifested as "a consuming fire" on Mt. Sinai (Exodus 24:16); as a
cloud that covered the Tent of Meeting and filled the tabernacle (Exodus 40:34);
and as a presence filling the entire earth (Isaiah 6:3). In the life of Jesus Christ,
the glory of God was fully present: at his birth the angels were surrounded by
God's glory (Luke 2:9); in becoming flesh, God's true likeness and splendor was
fully revealed (John 1:14); and at his transfiguration, Jesus manifested the glory
of God (Luke 9:32). In the life of the world, God's incomparable glory will be
ultimately revealed. This promise is the source of our hope. (Romans 8:18)

Patmos, a small island off the southwest coast of Asia Minor (Turkey), was
the place where John received the revelation of Jesus Christ, the visions con-
tained in the book of Revelation.

THE SEARCH BEGINS

What was *The Hope* of the early church? These passages will help you discover answers to that question. As you read make notes that indicate the type of
hope given. Copy verses that give *you* hope. Do not become preoccupied
with the symbolism present in the passages that are apocalyptic. Instead, use
these questions to focus your search:

- *What hope did Jesus offer for the future?*
- *What was Paul's attitude toward the future?*
- *What are some visions of promise and hope within the Revelation to John?*

Matthew 25:31–46, The Last Judgment

Mark 13:1–37, Watch!

Romans 8:18–39, The Future Glory

1 Corinthians 15:50–58, Victory in Christ

1 Thessalonians 4:13–5:11, Be Ready!

Revelation 1:1–20, John's Vision

Revelation 21:1–6, All Things New!

Revelation 22:1–7, Jesus is Coming Soon!

THE SEARCH CONTINUES

In these readings I have questions about...

In these readings I discovered...

FOCUSING THE SEARCH

Imagine combining all of the pictures of hope in the New Testament! What a tremendous mural of God's ultimate victory! Each vision of hope found in the twenty-seven books adds another part to the ultimate vision. Sometimes there is a temptation to focus too much attention upon the total mural. In the following exercise you can examine just a few pictures of hope from the larger panorama of the future glory of God.

Review the following passages from this session and answer the questions under them:

Matthew 25:31–46

What is God going to do?_____

_____

What hope does this passage give to you? _____

_____

Romans 8:26–39

What is God going to do?_____

_____

What hope does this passage give to you? _____

_____

1 Corinthians 15:50–58

What is God going to do?_____

_____

What hope does this passage give to you? _____

_____

Revelation 21:1–6

What is God going to do?_____

_____

What hope does this passage give to you? _____

_____

PUTTING IT TOGETHER

Just as Genesis provided answers to the questions of our ancestors, the visions and expressions of hope in the New Testament provided answers to questions the early Christians asked about the future. Today we still wonder about the future. Even though the future remains a mystery, what we do know and have experienced gives us an intense hope. The visions of Jesus, Paul, and John, while not answering all of our questions, sustain us in hope.

Using the information you have gained about hope in this Discovery, write a message to a family member or friend explaining the confidence you feel about the future in Christ.

REFLECTION

1. Consider Jesus' words:

...for I was hungry and you gave me food, I was thirsty and you gave me something to drink, I was a stranger and you welcomed me, I was naked and you gave me clothing, I was sick and you took care of me, I was in prison and you visited me. (Matthew 25:35–36)

Why do you think Jesus linked our present actions with the future judgment? What is the hope expressed in these words? In what ways do these words make a difference in your life? How does your hope in God's future affect your life today?

2. Reflect upon your search to know God through an understanding of the Bible. What hopes have been fulfilled as the result of this study?

The symbol for *The Goal* is the open Bible with the descending dove (the Holy Spirit) kindling the reader's understanding.

DISCOVERY 30

The Goal

THE STORY CONTINUES

I know what it is to have little, and I know what it is to have plenty. In any and all circumstances I have learned the secret of being well-fed and of going hungry, of having plenty and of being in need. I can do all things through him who strengthens me. Philippians 4:12–13

Notice that even though we have come to the end of this course, the section is not entitled "The Story Concludes." Following the events recorded in the New Testament, God's loving search for humanity continues. Throughout the centuries, as the good news of Jesus Christ spreads around the world, the story continues. In our day, as children, youth, and adults discover the transforming message of God's love, the story continues.

Paul's growth in faith provides a key for examining our own growth. Imprisoned and nearing the end of his life, Paul looks toward the goal – knowing Christ and sharing in his death and resurrection. He writes to the church in Philippi with words of encouragement, expressions of gratitude, and anticipation of the goal that awaits. In his victorious words there is hope for our journeys.

PREPARING FOR THE SEARCH

These definitions are important in your study of *The Goal*.

Epaphroditus (e-paf'roh-di'tuhs) was sent to Rome by the church at Philippi with gifts for Paul, who was in prison. While there, Epaphroditus became gravely ill. In his letter to the Philippians, Paul thanks the church for sending him, praises him, explains his illness, and asks them to receive him back with joy.

Euodia (yoo-oh'dee-uh) **and Syntyche** (sin'ti-kee), members of the church at Philippi, were involved in a personal dispute. Paul urges them to settle their differences as Christians.

Philippi was the location of the first European church founded by Paul. Early converts were Lydia and the Philippian jailer. (Acts 16:11–40)

Philippians. Written during one of Paul's imprisonments sometime between 54 and 62 A.D., this joy-filled letter to the church at Philippi recounts the progress of the gospel and his personal growth. Some scholars, pointing to the "roughness" of the letter's organization, believe that it contains the contents of two or three letters Paul sent to the church. In spite of great peril his mood is confident.

THE SEARCH BEGINS

As you read the passages listed below, you will discover why Paul was filled with joy. Take notes that will help you summarize the content of the various portions of the letter to the Philippians. These questions can help guide your reading:

- *What problems concern Paul?*
- *How does Paul affirm his belief that "all things work together for good for those who love God..." (Romans 8:28) in this letter?*
- *What causes Paul to rejoice?*
- *How does Paul's goal compare with your goal?*

Philippians 1:1–11, A Prayer for Fellow Christians

Philippians 1:12–30, To Live is Christ

Philippians 2:1–11, Imitate Christ!

Philippians 2:12–30, God Works in You

Philippians 3:1–11, To Know Christ

Philippians 3:12–4:1, Toward the Goal

Philippians 4:2–9, Always Rejoice!

Philippians 4:10–23, Strength for Every Circumstance

THE SEARCH CONTINUES

In these readings I have questions about...

In these readings I discovered...

FOCUSING THE SEARCH

Instead of selections from various books of the Bible, you have read all of Paul's letter to the Philippians. Toward the end of his letter, Paul reflects on what he has learned through the varied experiences of his life and ministry. Read again Philippians 4:10–13 to discover what Paul has learned. Then, write a short letter to someone you know expressing what *you* have learned as you have grown in faith. Include some information about what you have discovered about God and about yourself as a part of this course. Try using the same format Paul used:

Dear _____,

I have learned...

I know...

I have learned...

PUTTING IT TOGETHER

Your discovery of the Bible began thirty sessions ago with *The Search*. This final Discovery is a good time to evaluate the ways your reading, understanding, and reflecting have changed. Return to Discovery 1 and choose one or more of the Scripture passages to read again. Once again, take notes as you read. Then compare these notes with the ones you took before. What stands out now? What did you miss the first time? What greater understanding have you gained?

Rather than *The Goal*, this Discovery could also be entitled *The Search*. With a greater awareness of the exciting opportunities for further study that lie before you in the BIble, what do you hope to search for next as you continue to grow in faith?

REFLECTION

1. Reflect upon Paul's encouragement to "Rejoice in the Lord always." (Philippians 4:4) What makes you "rejoice in the Lord?"

Where in your life do you find it difficult to rejoice?

2. Paul was pressing toward "the goal for the prize of the heavenly call of God in Christ Jesus." (Philippians 3:14) What steps are you taking to reach your goal? As you press on, what are your sources of guidance and strength?